ALL THE MONEY
IN THE WORLD

ALSO BY LAURA VANDERKAM

168 Hours

ALL THE MONEY IN THE WORLD

What the Happiest People Know
About Getting and Spending

LAURA VANDERKAM

PORTFOLIO / PENGUIN

PORTFOLIO / PENGUIN
Published by the Penguin Group
Penguin Group (USA) Inc., 375 Hudson Street,
New York, New York 10014, U.S.A.
Penguin Group (Canada), 90 Eglinton Avenue East, Suite 700,
Toronto, Ontario, Canada M4P 2Y3
(a division of Pearson Penguin Canada Inc.)
Penguin Books Ltd, 80 Strand, London WC2R 0RL, England
Penguin Ireland, 25 St Stephen's Green, Dublin 2, Ireland
(a division of Penguin Books Ltd)
Penguin Books Australia Ltd, 250 Camberwell Road, Camberwell,
Victoria 3124, Australia
(a division of Pearson Australia Group Pty Ltd)
Penguin Books India Pvt Ltd, 11 Community Centre, Panchsheel Park,
New Delhi – 110 017, India
Penguin Group (NZ), 67 Apollo Drive, Rosedale, Auckland 0632,
New Zealand (a division of Pearson New Zealand Ltd)
Penguin Books (South Africa) (Pty) Ltd, 24 Sturdee Avenue,
Rosebank, Johannesburg 2196, South Africa

Penguin Books Ltd, Registered Offices:
80 Strand, London WC2R 0RL, England

First published in 2012 by Portfolio / Penguin,
a member of Penguin Group (USA) Inc.

1   3   5   7   9   10   8   6   4   2

LIBRARY OF CONGRESS CATALOGING-IN-PUBLICATION DATA

Vanderkam, Laura.
All the money in the world : what the happiest people know about getting and spending / Laura Vanderkam.
p. cm.
Includes bibliographical references and index.
ISBN 978-1-59184-457-0 (hardback)
1. Finance, Personal. 2. Money. 3. Happiness. I. Title.
HG179.V365 2012
332.024—dc23
2011036152

Printed in the United States of America
Set in Baskerville Std
Designed by Jaime Putorti

While the author has made every effort to provide accurate telephone numbers and Internet addresses at the time of publication, neither the publisher nor the author assumes any responsibility for errors, or for changes that occur after publication. Further, the publisher does not have any control over and does not assume any responsibility for author or third-party Web sites or their content.

CONTENTS

ALL THE MONEY IN THE WORLD

THE HOW TO BUY HAPPINESS HANDBOOK

ALL THE MONEY
IN THE WORLD

You Have More Money Than You Think

One Saturday afternoon, as I was skimming digests of the e-mail lists I subscribe to, a curious headline on a parenting list caught my eye: "The sudden acquisition of wealth."

With a title like that, I had to read more. Early that morning, a long-time subscriber had posted that a major tech company—which you've definitely heard of—had just acquired her husband's employer. In order to keep key employees around and happy during the transition, the deep-pocketed buyer had offered them various monetary incentives, including raises, stock options, and retention bonuses. The poster kept mum on the exact dollar figure, but she did announce that, thanks to this windfall, she and her husband were now joining the ranks of the rich.

She went on to add that the two of them had always lived modestly—in her opinion, perhaps too modestly—with weekends consumed by comparison shopping trips to grocery stores in order to find the best deals. Like most people who spend their days figuring out how to save a buck or two, she had long fantasized about how they'd live if they had enough money. Now they did.

So what was the best way to use it? "The kids' college accounts are underfunded and we can remedy that," she wrote. "We already take nice vacations—the problem we're running into there is limits on time. But what else can we do with it?"

Despite sending this message on a weekend, she soon received a flurry of e-mails from other subscribers, all of whom were eager to share their own ideas. Some were wise (consult a financial planner). Some were more offbeat ("buy gold coins and a small safe"). Some urged the couple to save for the future and for rainy months, the post-2009 version of rainy days. But this thrifty couple had already paid off their mortgage and carried no other debts. Living within their means and saving were deeply ingrained habits for them, ones they needed no reminder to keep up.

And so the conversation soon became more philosophical. Instead of figuring out what to do with the money, people started thinking of what the money would allow her to do. Over the years, this woman had shared some of her career frustrations with the other subscribers on the list. Perhaps, another poster suggested, her newfound wealth could be an opportunity to rethink what she wanted to do professionally. Others suggested she could be more generous with the causes she cared about, an idea she liked though she had trouble thinking of herself as a philanthropist. Another subscriber shared the rather wistful story of how her parents, who had accumulated massive amounts of wealth, never let themselves spend any of it. When they passed away, she'd inherited a nice sum and, not wanting to repeat her parents' example, was spending the money on first-class travel and charitable projects she thought her parents would have supported. She was glad for these opportunities. But she couldn't help feeling sad that her parents never got to experience any of the pleasures their wealth could have bought. After all, no matter how much or how little we have, none of us will have it forever.

Despite the diversity of tips this newly rich woman received, the overwhelming response leads us to one incontrovertible truth: money is a powerful thing. It is also complicated. The more we think about it, the more it leads us to ask questions: "How can I get it? Should I save it or spend it? If I spend it, what should I spend it on?" For all we may say "money can't buy happiness" or dismiss its importance in our lives, it must mean something to us. Otherwise why would so many people take time from their weekend to share their thoughts on the subject with a woman they knew mostly through an e-mail list?

One reason we think about money so much is that it provides an easy way to compare ourselves to others, and we humans are obsessed with how we stack up against our peers. New science is showing that we may even be wired to defer to symbols of wealth and status (real or perceived). A handful of Dutch researchers once set up a test at a shopping mall where a woman asked passersby to answer survey questions. When she wore a sweater with a conspicuous Tommy Hilfiger label, shoppers were more likely to take the survey than when she wore an identical sweater with no logo. In a separate study, the researchers had volunteers watch a video of a man being interviewed for a job. When he wore a designer logo, people rated him as more qualified and recommended a higher salary than when he didn't. Even an experiment by the same researchers, which sent women door-to-door to collect money for charity, revealed that people would give twice as much per answered door when the women wore designer logos as when they wore something generic.

Clearly, this is silly. Indeed, our conscious minds know such status symbols are meaningless (not to mention easily faked), which is why we spout so many aphorisms denigrating our money obsession: "You can't judge a book by its cover" or "Money is the root of all evil." We bemoan a materialistic society (which seems to encompass everyone but ourselves). We tell whoever will listen that we must be morally superior to those rich types we read about or see on TV, that those people must have sold their souls to achieve such sums or else are harboring some secret misery. But meanwhile, many of us stick with work we don't enjoy because "it pays the bills"—another moral compromise, if you think about it, albeit one more socially sanctioned.

So what are we to make of this? Basically, that our beliefs about money are muddled. We shouldn't be surprised. The burgeoning field of happiness research is showing that we're bad at guessing what will bring us satisfaction in many spheres of life. One classic example from the literature is a study comparing people with serious kidney disease—who had to spend hours every week tethered to dialysis machines—with healthy people. Looking at that situation, you'd assume the dialysis patients would be miserable. But they weren't. On the whole, they weren't unhappier than their healthier peers. We get used to many things, and as a corollary, can convince ourselves we should be unhappy despite all manner of objective blessings. You can have a wonderful job, a loving family, great health, and still be in a bad mood because you spilled coffee on your shirt when you slammed on the brakes because someone cut you off in traffic on the way to work. Happiness, we are learning, is the result of conscious choices.

But, when it comes to money, our choices are often the opposite. For all the obsession regarding our net worth, most of us fail to consider our decisions rationally, and in the end we succumb to one, essentially universal, basic financial assumption:

There is never enough.

This is the assumption that the woman on my e-mail list held until her husband's big raise made that impossible to continue believing. We've all done this, lamenting the things we'd do if only we had "all the money in the world . . . ," dismissing such grand ideas and desires as fantasy as we adopt more fatalistic attitudes of what responsible people should do with their resources.

For instance, if you believe various online budget calculators, prudent people should spend the bulk of their incomes staving off the demons of homelessness, starvation, and nakedness. People make wildly varying amounts, and human needs are relatively basic, so it seems strange that we should all spend 5 percent on clothing, 15 percent on transportation, 10–15 percent on food, and 25–35 percent on housing. Yet these are the percentages that pop up again and again. Many of these budgets leave a mere 5–10 percent for that category known as "miscellaneous"—which is where most of the fun stuff occurs—whether we earn $40,000, $400,000, or $4 million.

But this idea is not gospel. As often as we listen to the assumed expertise of the crowd, no one is forcing us to earn or spend our money in certain ways, and when we step back, we may realize that the resources we already have or can obtain can do more for our happiness than we think.

As I've been examining the way we earn and spend our money, and how we can all do so better, I've started asking people an even grander version of the question from that e-mail list:

If you had all the money in the world—not literally, but all you wanted—what would you change about your life?

The answers people give are fascinating. They start with obvious annoyances: "I would stop commuting." "I would never empty the dishwasher again." "I would only fly business class and scoot to the front of obnoxious security lines." Then they ponder the more aspirational: "I would work less and travel more." A few people blithely claim to be so blissful that they wouldn't change anything about their personal lives, but if pressed they soon realize they could change their lives by instead using that money to improve other people's lives. They begin contemplating how they would change the world, doing philanthropy aimed at injustices that rile them and investing in ventures that would help create a world in which they'd want to live.

Or, on the lighter side, as one woman told me, "I would buy a couple of networks and cable channels and cancel all reality shows."

I find this exercise clarifying. For starters, it makes us realize that our biggest vexations might be solvable with far less than all the money in the world. If you hate emptying the dishwasher, you may be able to bribe a teenager into emptying it for a price you're willing to pay. You could use paper plates and write a check to your favorite environmental charity as atonement. Even a business-class-only travel schedule would involve an earthbound (if large) sum. More important, though, by figuring out what matters to you, you can start to figure out ways you might be able to use money in a satisfying fashion. If working less and traveling more is important to you, then over time, it can become a financial goal. Vast amounts of money already come in and out of our lives, and could be redeployed if we wished.

That's what Danny and Jillian Tobias discovered. This young couple worked hard for five years right out of school, living on one salary and saving the other by sharing a very cheap one-bedroom apartment in Washington, D.C. They drove a hand-me-down car on weekends and used public transportation during the week. They went mountain biking and kayaking rather than barhopping, and had friends over rather than going out much. None of this involved depriving themselves ("really, it wasn't so hard," Danny reports), but despite paying off student loans at the same time, they managed to build up $80,000 in savings over that half decade. They then used that cash to travel the world for two straight years. They climbed Mount Kilimanjaro. They saw the mountain gorillas in Uganda. They traveled along the old Silk Road overland from Istanbul to China, and sampled as many local beers as possible through the Americas. "Part of us wanted to keep saving for five more years and just retire to an expat lifestyle instead of taking the two years off," Danny says. But, "we decided that didn't work for us, we wanted to have kids one day." If they put off their "mini-retirement" they weren't sure when they'd do it.

They've now come back to the United States to start their adult lives—without much capital, of course. As they traveled, "we made it a policy to err on the side of spending the cash rather than saving it," Danny says, but their low bank balance is hardly a different situation from that faced by the average person in her late 20s. Many people could do what Danny and Jillian did if they wanted. The difference is that, rather than spend 35 percent of their income on a house they didn't want or need, the Tobias family asked how they could use money to build the lives they want. By doing so, they forced themselves out of the scarcity mind-set, the notion that the resources to do, have, and experience the things most people dream about will always be elusive.

All the Money in the World is about the link between money and happiness, and about how money can be used in our rich society to optimize well-being for ourselves and those we care about. To start, we must stop thinking about money as something evil or soulless, or something that is interesting only in terms of how our pile compares to our neighbors'. Instead, we have to start thinking of it as a tool, a means to acquiring, doing, and taking care of things that bring us joy. I've come to believe that people who are happiest about money operate under three premises of wealth, a word that has less to do with quantity than with outlook:

1. I have enough. There are some people in this world who have more, but also plenty with less.

2. If I want more than I have now to achieve big goals, I can figure out a way to get it.

3. Every dollar is a choice. How I earn it and spend it are up to me.

I was pondering these premises soon after I started working on this book, when my husband, Michael, and I took our first kidless vacation in ages. Shortly after Christmas 2010, we ventured to Morocco, which is far from the poorest country in the world but certainly not the richest. Parts are well developed, with vast mineral resources paying for miles of freeway so new that our GPS system was puzzled. Other parts, however, feature roads that are little more than tracks through the hills, and in many rural areas, people live in the same subsistence goat-farming style that their ancestors did centuries ago. The children in these small villages looked shorter than they should be—sometimes like toddlers though they were walking to school—but stunted growth is inevitable in pockets of even a middle-income country where people live on less than $2 a day.

Such a subsistence life has many difficulties, and so people often flee those villages to try to make money off tourists in ways that I, as a tourist, definitely had mixed feelings about. Along the mountainous road from Marrakech to Ouarzazate, men appeared around every bend selling volcanic rocks with crystals inside. They'd have little inventory but would stand beside the road all day hawking what they had. Maybe some people enjoy standing beside a dusty highway selling rocks, but more likely the reason they stood there is that getting one tourist to overpay for rocks produces a better living than anything else they could be doing.

When adults sell useless objects, that's one thing. What's more disturbing is when adults send children to capitalize on visitors—selling packets of tissues, as one little girl kept attempting in the main square of Marrakech, or hassling us to let them be our guides by the Ouarzazate old city. Many of these children and teens were at least trilingual (Arabic, French, English), but despite having a skill set that would put them well on their way to getting a job at the UN, they were carrying tourists' bags. This is an appalling waste of human capital, one that I have seen in way too many other places—such as

Cambodia, where I once overheard children ask a Japanese couple for money in their language, then turn and do the same in English to me. In India, which exports some of the most driven and talented workers in the world, the Delhi slums have burned images in my brain of children picking through garbage dumps alongside dogs, competing for anything that could be used or sold.

Few of us in the developed world, even if we're struggling through recessions or more ongoing woes, can fathom sending our young children out to sell tissues to strangers or scavenge in a garbage dump. That should make the first premise of wealth obvious. Even with purchasing power parity conversions, modest wages in the United States would go a long way in Morocco, Cambodia, or India.

It is human nature to compare ourselves with people who have more, and hence to fret that we're somehow behind—that if we're perfectly comfortable we should be millionaires, and if we're millionaires we should be billionaires—but it's just as easy to compare ourselves with those who have less. Indeed, it's easier, because there are a lot more of them. According to 2006 figures from the UN's World Institute for Development Economics Research, one needs household assets of about $61,000 to be in the top 10 percent of the wealthiest people worldwide. The median net worth of the world— the point at which half the population is below—was only about $2,200. In 2007, the median net worth for U.S. households was about $120,000.

If that thought makes you feel rich, why just compare your wealth to people alive today? Four hundred years ago, King Louis XIV with all his riches didn't have access to the antibiotics, vaccines, or modern dentistry we take for granted. Maria Theresa, head of the entire Habsburg empire for 40 years in the 1700s, saw 6 of her 16 children die before adulthood, a ratio that few parents of any income level in the developed world could fathom now. Anyone who's been born in a developed country in the past 70 years has pretty much won the lottery of human history. We are among the richest people who have ever walked this planet, and if you are part of the demographic that has the income to buy books like this and the education to read them, then you have won a second time. Because—looking at the second premise of wealth—if people around the world who have not been for-tunate enough to receive the same level of schooling as we have can figure out how to add to their resources by selling rocks, presumably we can figure out ways to expand our circumstances over time as well.

So if we've won the lottery of human history, even if not the Pow-erball version, what should we do with the winnings? This brings us to premise three. They say money can't buy happiness, but that's an incomplete story. For starters, I'm not sure I'd repeat that aphorism to the Moroccan mother forced to send her daughter out to sell tissues so the family can eat. At its core, money is just a means of exchange, there to satisfy needs and desires. Compared with much of humanity, we have quite a bit of this tool, and operating from this mind-set of plenty we can recognize that earning and spending decisions are, to a large degree, choices. Beyond fulfilling our basic needs—which some people such as Danny and Jillian Tobias manage to do for quite low amounts, even in the United States—whenever we spend a dollar on one thing we are choosing not to spend it on something else. Each money decision says something about a person's values (even the value that you don't believe in committing tax evasion). For instance, even if you had all the money you wanted, I'm sure you could list several items or experiences that would bring you no pleasure whatsoever. I often feel this way looking at pictures from avant-garde fashion shows. So perhaps we should change that tired phrase. If money can't buy happiness, perhaps we're not spending it right.

———————

Money is a well-worn topic, so I want to clarify what this book is and is not. The best way to think of it is as a series of essays on intriguing money topics, aimed at making the reader say "I'd never thought of it that way before." Unlike many writers of money books, I'm not going to tell you what a mutual fund is, or which you should invest in. I'm not going to share my secret for making millions in real estate, mostly because I haven't made millions in real estate. I won't tell you how credit bureaus calculate your FICO score; I can't say I entirely understand it, though they seem to smile on paying your bills in full and on time, which sounds like a good idea to me, too. Perhaps most important, there is nothing in this book on getting out of debt. While you can operate from a mind-set of plenty if you have just a few more dollars coming in per month than you have going out for your family's basic needs, it is hard to have this mind-set when every dollar and more is already spoken for. Over time any situation can be changed. But several excellent books on that topic already exist, and I can't add anything new there.

As I've read those books, though, I've noticed a repeating narrative: pay off your nonmortgage debts, thus freeing up $500 or so per month to invest. The reason you should do this, the story goes, is that if you put that cash in the stock market, in funds returning 12 percent a year, in 40 years, you'll have $5.7 million saved up. That's a compelling calculation, if a little dubious, but even if you take these claims at face value, here's something these books don't mention: there's a lot of life between your last $500 debt payment and having $5.7 million in your brokerage account. How should you earn and spend your money in the meantime? How should you make day-to-day decisions and big long-term decisions about your job, your house, your car, your family, and anything else that is important to you?

This book is for people who want to be mindful about their financial choices—who want to question what the logo on the sweater of that smiling woman in the mall means. It is for people who want to think and plan ahead, who are interested in how people earn and spend their money now and have done so in the past, and how we can all do it better. I'll try to be practical when possible, but I also think it's more interesting to think broadly, to move beyond pure self-help to the larger questions of why we do what we do. Many personal finance books assume that a golf-intensive retirement is a universal goal, but should it be? The real estate industry assumes everyone wants to stretch to own a home, because it's a wise investment—though the past few years have shown the flaws of that notion, and it's unclear that houses make people happy. Frugality tomes assume that housing and transportation costs are fixed, and so they focus on variable costs such as groceries or car insurance, even though these are relatively small percentages of the average family's budget. As for that whole "budget" idea? I believe it needs a rethink, too. I'm a freelance writer who has never made the same amount month to month. And so the notion that there is some set figure coming in that then has to be divvied up according to certain percentages doesn't seem inevitable to me either. A growing proportion of the population is in the same boat, and partly for this reason, it's sometimes easier, and less painful, to think about earning more rather than spending less. I'll look at certain assumptions about what it costs to raise kids, at the few categories of spending that do correlate with happiness, and the opportunity cost involved with saving money by sacrificing time. I'll discuss how to give money away and how to use it to create opportunities for other people.

In my previous book, *168 Hours*, I wrote that I was not a time management guru. I'm often not even a particularly sparkling example of time management, as one audience in Pittsburgh must have discovered, savoring the irony, as their time management speaker rushed in disheveled and five minutes late. I came at the topic of time as a journalist who likes to write about economics with a human angle. How do people optimize the allocation of resources? Time is a resource. So is money, with some intriguing parallels and differences. I want to approach the topic of money in the same way I analyzed time, asking big questions of what we do with it, while making the subject more entertaining with the stories of foragers, mega-families, anti-lawn crusaders, microphilanthropy entrepreneurs, preachers with a money-back guarantee on tithing, and others who can teach us something about money, even if none of us are actual CPAs or financial planners.

This is not a book about me, though I will sometimes appear in the narrative. One major reason this topic intrigued me was the opportunity to learn to be a better steward of the resources I have or can muster. If I have been lucky in life to have enough, what should I do to build a life that is worthy of that fortune? Even people with far more money than I could ever hope to accumulate eventually have to make choices. So what choice framework can optimize well-being, both in my own life and for those I care about?

It's a challenging question, one I hope you will ask as well, as you read this book. After surveying the research on maximizing happiness, I have some concrete suggestions to add to that e-mail discussion on sudden wealth. These days, I buy more little pleasures like lattes and flowers, and spend more on gifts and on getting together with friends. I spend more on something when I can identify the specific proprietor or creative type who would benefit from my purchase. On the other hand, we made the choice while I was writing this book to move to Pennsylvania from New York City, in part for the lower cost of living. My husband and I flew to Morocco on a cheaper flight than we'd originally intended. I used a chunk of the cash we saved to make a donation to a rural—and partially solar-powered!—library building project in the Zawiya Ahansal region near some of the villages we passed through. In this part of Morocco, 70 percent of men and 90 percent of women are illiterate. This library will be the first access ever for the region's 15,000 inhabitants to books, newspapers, and the Internet. I hope in some small way that helps to create a world where little girls don't need to sell tissues and grown-ups don't need to sell rocks unless they find it fulfilling to do so. I quite enjoy picturing Moroccan kids at those computers. Much more than I would have enjoyed giving that cash to Delta. As this and many other experiences have taught me, when you think broadly about the options, money can buy happiness.

This book is about how to do just that.

CHAPTER 1

What Else Could That Ring Buy?

I n late December 2009, a young man e-mailed me with an unusual request. He wanted to propose to his girlfriend in front of the LOVE sculpture in midtown Manhattan and thought it would be nice to hire some singers from the choir I was then managing to serenade the unsuspecting lady. As we exchanged e-mails about the song, our formation, and when we could meet for coffee so I could recognize him on the street, we got to talking about weddings and, as often happens, the massive expenditures associated with them. A few weeks into our correspondence, he picked up the lovely diamond ring he'd selected for his bride-to-be. It felt strange to hand over money he'd been saving for two years to pay for a piece of jewelry, he told me, but it was for a good cause.

Certainly, marrying the love of his life was a worthwhile endeavor. As my fellow choir members and I sang on that cold street corner, though, and cheered when his beloved accepted, I couldn't help but ponder the other half of this young man's statement. When you think about it, it *is* strange to hand over such a large chunk of one's savings for a rock. A dazzling rock, to be sure, and one that you hope the eventual owner will wear for the rest of her life. But given that most of us have a hard time saving that long for anything, it's odd that we don't think more about why we spend so much on small amounts of pressurized carbon—something the wedding industry claims more than 80 percent of U.S. couples do. According to statistics from TheKnot.com's annual Real Weddings survey, the average couple spent $5,392 on an engagement ring in 2010.

So why do we buy diamonds? As we ponder the topics of money, life, and happiness, I think it's worth exploring the logic behind this near-universal purchase, and what it says about our usual money decisions. The most curious part of the whole equation is that the five grand that couples spend on rings, and indeed, the whole $20,000-plus that the average couple spends on the wedding, is spent before the marriage begins, when the relationship is still gleaming as bright as that shiny rock on the bride's finger. Unfortunately, people being the way they are, that gleam will dull a bit for most folks in the years after a couple says "I do." Over the decades, kids, jobs, and chores will conspire to drain a couple's emotional bank account. It is then that they start daydreaming about all the things they would do to put some passion and enjoyment back into their marriage, if only they had the cash (and time).

What we forget in all this is that money is perfectly fungible. It is as easily spent on one thing as another. Few young couples ponder this as they plan the weddings that usher in their lives together, but in the later, more frazzled days that will inevitably come, the same money spent on rings and elaborate cakes could be invested quite strategically in making them live happily after. How strategically? That is, what else could that ring buy?

You can buy a lot of things for $5,392, but I like this question because it highlights the concept of opportunity cost and what it means to use our resources wisely. This is a line of thought that has become increasingly prevalent as the economy limps out of the doldrums of the past few years. Of course, pundits have oversold the new sobriety, as they always do. One of my favorite pastimes is finding quotes from old financial magazines that completely misjudge human nature. Like this gem from *Money*, published about a year after the Black Friday crash of 1987: "The period of great permissive spending, the narcissism, the idea that you could speculate in stocks without risk—that's all over now." Sure, if by "all over now" you mean "over until the Nasdaq inflates like a balloon from 1997 to 1999." Still, I believe there is something worth exploring in this post–Great Recession desire to align our money with our values. Even when our wallets fatten back up again, wouldn't it be nice to know we're making each dollar count? Few couples basking in the glow of early romance consider the practical side of what all that wedding cash could buy them, and there are plenty of emotional reasons we don't question an expense so deeply ingrained in our culture that we might as well stop celebrating the Fourth of July while we're at it. But doing so creates an interesting thought experiment—one we can extend to all our money decisions—and brings up evidence that perhaps the way we handle our money is more of a choice than we think.

THE BAUBLE ECONOMY

For all the time brides spend planning their weddings, few spend many minutes pondering how diamond rings became so ubiquitous in the first place. The answer turns out to be a fascinating story of changing social standards and blatant opportunism. Betrothal rings have been around for a while, but the popular diamond obsession appears to have had its genesis in the 1930s. In a 1990 article for the *Journal of Law, Economics, & Organization*, legal professor Margaret Brinig argued that rings became popular when states repealed their laws allowing women to sue for "breach of promise to marry." While premarital sex was still a no-no in the years after World War I, there was some gray area, and close to half of women lost their virginity while engaged. "All this was well and good," Brinig wrote, but for the woman, "if the marriage never came about, she was irretrievably barred from offering an unblemished self to a new suitor and suffered a loss in 'market value.'" A crafty man wishing to have sex with nice girls could "propose" and then jilt a string of fiancées. Perhaps to guard against this threat, multiple states had laws on the books allowing women to sue for breach of promise, thus dissuading men from such behavior, or at least making them face expensive consequences for any casual trysts.

Then, in 1935, a legislator from Indiana sponsored a bill abolishing broken engagement as a reason to sue for damages. Other jurisdictions followed, which soon raised a question: if a woman couldn't sue, what could she do to protect herself? One solution would be to demand a large transfer of capital as part of an engagement. That would make any prospective grooms think twice about seducing a woman under false pretenses. The most efficient way to do this would be for the man to give his beloved money. Money can be used for anything, and so this method would at least let the woman do something useful with it, like go to school or start a business. But genteel folks have always found cash a bit tacky in proper situations, so that didn't catch on.

Fortuitously, at the same time brides were looking for something expensive yet respectable to secure their honor, the diamond industry faced a glut of the precious stones and needed some way to move them. Seeing an opportunity, the DeBeers company staged one of the first national marketing campaigns to boost diamond sales. Its advertising agency got Hollywood stars to wear conspicuous rings, and movies soon featured engagement scenes involving diamonds. Within just three decades the diamond engagement ring was welded into the culture, almost universally accepted, and soon subject to rampant inflation as "two months' salary" became the suggested tax on grooms, and in certain quarters anything less than a carat—close to the average now—became a cause for furtive whispers about the man's finances. Because humans are wired to defer to markers of status, men like my young friend face enormous pressure to spend big in pursuit of rings that make their brides look well cared for.

Of course, the ring is only the first major matrimonial purchase in a long cascade of spending. Any merchant knows that once a customer buys one expensive item, the floodgates open. Why not buy nice floor mats if you've already bought the car? With our appetites for luxury whetted by pricey diamond rings, it's easy to justify myriad other purchases that you'd probably never spring for at other points in your life. Back when I was planning my wedding in spring and summer of 2004, I amassed quite a collection of *Martha Stewart Weddings* magazines and wedding planning books. I spent hours pondering questions like whether we needed matchbooks with our names and our wedding date on them. Did I want our guests to blow bubbles or wave sparklers or throw confetti? The intervening years have not changed the wedding industry's opinion that these small and inevitably expensive details should consume a bride's focus. Popping over to The Knot's wedding shop recently, and scrolling past obvious categories such as dresses, I soon came across more curious items such as "Clear Diamond-shaped Table Jewels," billed as "beautifully faceted and shimmering," there to "add luxe glamour to your wedding decor" or "whimsical flair to an engagement party." Most items can be personalized. For instance, you can get a "personalized elegant square platter and easel" (for displaying table numbers) for $64, and 100 personalized Hershey's Kisses for $19.99—or about four times what nonpersonalized Kisses would go for in the grocery store.

The little stuff is neither here nor there. We've all spent money on our own equivalents of table jewels—or even more pointless things.

In my case, T-Mobile late fees come to mind. But the net effect of all this choosing or not choosing personalized Hershey's Kisses is to distract the mind with so many minor things that the wedding, not the marriage, becomes the point. The process becomes less about pledging lifelong devotion and monogamy to another person, and more about whether you'll have toile on the seats on that one perfect day.

We go there willingly, and our culture does little to reject this mind-set. When a couple announces they're engaged, the first thing everyone wants to do is ooh and ah over her diamond, even though with modern sexual mores, it seems quaint to think that a man would need to transfer capital to a woman to ensure that she won't be "ruined" by sex during engagement. In the media frenzy leading up to Prince William and Kate Middleton's wedding in April 2011, magazines devoted entire spreads to the coach she would ride in to the church—and almost no real estate to how the royal couple intended to raise their children or what they'd do with themselves after the nuptials. We go there because, in the popular imagination, a wedding is the culmination of decades of dreams. For the bride it is her day. She gets to be a princess—another reason we are so obsessed with royal weddings that involve real princesses. It's a child's fantasy, and so the tendency is to think of a wedding as a four-year-old would. That is, "once you find the person, you're always riding off into the sunset," says Alisa Bowman, author of *Project: Happily Ever After*, a memoir of her marriage. In fairy tales, the wedding comes right before "The End."

AFTER HAPPILY EVER AFTER

If you think about it, this wedding-as-ending concept is ridiculous. No matter how perfect your perfect day is, in real life you still have to get out of bed the next morning. You will come home from your honeymoon. You will go back to school or to work. And eventually, the snoring and possibly foul-breathed person you're waking up next to will do something to get on your nerves.

This is what Bowman discovered. She and her husband began their marriage as infatuated as all couples. Then, over the next eight years, they faced a colicky baby, her postpartum depression, two episodes of his unemployment, and so forth, all of which shoveled stress into their lives to the point where they were fighting over which groceries to buy and how to do laundry. She fantasized about him dropping dead. Indeed, she planned his funeral. In case he failed to die, however, she also reports that "I was fantasizing about divorce several times a day."

Bowman can cite stats that she's not unusual. She claims that 72 percent of married women have considered divorce, and more than half are bored in bed. We all love our kids, but even the most loving marriages will be strained by small children and the conflicts over housework, finances, and time that ensue. Marriage counselors see these same fights over and over again. They also prescribe very low-tech and well-known cures: time focused just on each other, time spent communicating, a commitment to easing the burdens of any party who feels overworked or underappreciated. Yet one *Redbook* poll found that 45 percent of its mostly mom readers had date night "pretty rarely." An additional 18 percent managed a regular date night just once a month. And forget a cleaning service. Who can afford that? Amid the diaper and grocery bills, the mortgage and health insurance co-pays, many couples feel as if there's just no money for luxuries or romantic extras.

Except once there was.

Remember those rings? With the same $5,392 the average couple spends on an engagement ring, a set of new parents could pay a babysitter $50 a night for 107 nights so they could have time to themselves or go neck in their car like teenagers.

The $12,124 The Knot reports the average couple spends on a reception venue could cover a $100 housecleaning service, twice a month, for the entire five years many two-kid couples spend in that sticky stage when children spill milk just to see what will happen.

The average $1,988 florist and decor bill could be doled out, instead, as 198 thinking-of-you $10 bouquets—a once-a-month gesture of love for a solid 16.5 years.

Indeed, the couple could elope, purchase a gigantic cubic zirconium ring to one-up the Joneses, and invest the whole $26,984 cost of a wedding in creating a "freedom fund" designed to give them more financial security and flexibility in their careers, long after the guests would have thrown out the Jordan almonds somebody decreed are a wedding necessity.

None of these calculations mean that spending big bucks on a wedding or ring is wrong. I would be a total hypocrite to claim that, and I'm quite happy with many of my biggest wedding expenditures from years ago, such as hiring my choir to sing at the ceremony. But I do think we can learn something from couples who stage grand celebrations on the cheap. Chris Rice, community director for Housing and Residential Life at Webster University in St. Louis, met his wife in graduate school. He wanted to propose, but "diamonds are expensive," he says, and "we didn't have that money to spend. We didn't want to go into debt for a ring." They talked about it and decided that "our love is good enough that it didn't have to be a diamond." He bought his fiancée a ring featuring a blue sapphire surrounded by two white sapphires and some intricate latticework. It is stunning and "pretty sizable. It's kind of hard not to notice," he says. "It's so unique that everyone comments on it." Total cost? $267, which included a lifetime warranty.

That philosophy persisted as they planned their October 1, 2010, wedding at the Butterfly House in St Louis. Realizing that no one actually likes fondant, they treated their guests to a sundae bar (total:

$100) rather than an elaborate cake. Since the wedding was outside in a naturally beautiful setting, they didn't have to spend much on flowers. By having the ceremony and the reception in the same spot, they saved on rental costs. And, of course, the biggest way to save is to share the day only with people you really want there. Often "you invite people because you feel like you have to invite them," says Rice. But "you really don't."

It's an intriguing idea. But my larger point for the young and betrothed—and for anyone, really—is that what people do with their money is a choice, and these choices reflect our priorities. If we sport diamond rings but claim we don't have money for date night, we are essentially saying that jewelry is worth more to us than spending quality time with our spouses. This hard truth continues through all the architecture of our lives. If we say we don't have time to hang out with our kids because we have to work to pay the mortgage, we are saying that the house is more important than our offspring. We can blow our cash on a showy car or save it to finance a transition into a dream career. Money spent on one thing is money not spent on something else, and these choices have consequences for our happiness and the happiness of those we vow to love. Consider this: many of us will spend four figures on wedding flowers and then not spend four figures on flowers for our spouses for the rest of our lives. We do this even though happiness research finds that small, frequent gestures have a greater impact on our overall well-being than bigger, infrequent events. You get used to having won the lottery, as one classic study from the 1970s of winners of the Illinois State Lottery discovered. You get used to being married, as a German study of 1,761 individuals who got and stayed married over 15 years found. Yet as Sonja Lyubomirsky, a professor of psychology at the University of California, Riverside, writes in her book *The How of Happiness: A Scientific Approach to Getting the Life You Want*, there can be significant variability in this adaptation. She describes one German study participant whose happiness boost from marriage lasted years past the usual decline. "He decided to dedicate himself to be the best husband he could be and not take his wife and their relationship for granted," she writes. "He consciously remembers to say 'I love you,' to bring her flowers, to initiate plans, trips, and hobbies, to take an interest in his wife's challenges, success, and feelings." Small repeated acts of consideration can keep love blooming years hence.

Indeed, this is how Bowman saved her marriage—learning to focus on her husband, to plan dates together, and otherwise invest energy in something that seems so easy when a diamond ring first slides onto a bride-to-be's finger. While planning a wedding is tough, "where the true hard work comes is afterward," she says. The babysitters and cleaning services that make such labor easier might not seem as romantic as toasting flutes and clear diamond-shaped table jewels, let alone a big rock in a Tiffany box. But in the long run, says Bowman, "the ring doesn't keep you together." A little profligate spending in a marriage just might.

THE RECKONING

This line of thought is just a microcosm of the broader concept of using money mindfully—nudging toward a better life by asking some version of the question "What else could that ring buy?"

What else could that rug buy?

What else could that sweater buy?

What else could that car payment buy?

Everything has an opportunity cost. Money is completely fungible, and so every penny spent on one thing could be spent on something else.

The question all of us need to ask ourselves is whether that something else might actually make us or our loved ones happier. In *168*

Hours, I encouraged people to keep a time log so they could get a clear sense of exactly how they were spending their hours and minutes. That way, they could analyze these patterns and see if they matched their priorities. Similarly, most financial counselors will tell anyone pondering their finances to track everything that's coming in and going out. It's a reasonable idea, and I know spending logs have their devotees. One friend of mine reports that he's kept a Quicken log of every dollar he's earned or spent since 1998. The U.S. Bureau of Labor Statistics (BLS) keeps a similar national spending log with the annual Consumer Expenditure Survey. According to the BLS, the average American household, with 1.3 wage earners supporting 2.5 people, took in $62,857 in 2009. After paying taxes, the average household then spent:

- ▸ $16,895 on housing

- ▸ $7,658 on transportation (including $1,986 on gas)

- ▸ $6,372 on food ($3,753 at home and $2,619 away)

- ▸ $5,471 on personal insurance and pensions

- ▸ $3,126 on health care

- ▸ $2,693 on entertainment

- ▸ $1,725 on apparel and services

- ▸ $5,127 on "other"

Of course, averages hide a great deal of variance. To see how you stack up against people more like you, go over to Bundle.com, a budgeting site that saves your data to compare it against that of millions of other users. There, we learn that in Minneapolis, a family with parents in their late 30s to early 40s, earning $75,000–$100,000 per year, spends $704 per month on getting around. A single young woman (18–25) living in San Francisco and making $40,000–$50,000 a year spends $1,091 per month on food and drink. In New York City, families with youngish parents and incomes over $125,000 spend $1,836 per year on phones.

Once you've laid out just how many dollars you bring in and how many you spend and on what, you might persuade yourself to use that money differently. Judi Rosenthal, a financial planner, tells me she used to pride herself on not owning a car, which was economical enough in New York City. Then she moved to Boston, where the public transportation coverage wasn't as thorough. A few bus snafus led to a few tardy appearances at work. To avoid that stress, and the massive financial hit that losing her job would entail, she began taking cabs whenever the weather fouled. This turned out to happen frequently in Boston. Eventually, she added up her cab fares for a month and realized she could save money by leasing a Honda Civic, even with paying for parking. That's saying something, given that leasing is usually not a great financial proposition.

However, my sense is that most people have a better grasp on their money than they do on their time, which gets logged regularly only when people get paid by the hour, and almost never in their personal lives. We have to account for our earnings with our taxes and our spending when we pay the bills, so these numbers are probably not total shocks. At least I hope they're not. I also know that, to many personal finance types, the brilliance of a spending log is that it points out how much money we're all "wasting" on little indulgences like coffee. While these categories can be trimmed if people have larger financial goals, sometimes small pleasures are a very affordable way to boost happiness in our lives. What else could that ring buy? An awful lot of lattes. Plus, this exercise is usually done to make sure that the "money coming in" category is bigger than the "money going out" category. I know this isn't always a given. But there are shelves of books written on the topic of clawing out of the hell that characterizes consumer debt. Let's say that, for you, the money coming in is more than the money going out. You are not spending $1,800 a month on something you were completely unaware of. Here are two more interesting questions:

1. **How do you feel about the money you're earning?** You probably feel something about the amount. One 2008 Gallup poll found that 51 percent of employed Americans felt underpaid, 46 percent felt they were fairly paid, and 3 percent felt they were overpaid. If you fit into the first category, spend some time pondering why, and whether you could, over time, change that. This is a subject we'll come back to in the next chapter. Whatever category you fall into, how do you feel about the way you're earning your money? Do you wake up wanting to go to work, or are you counting the days until retirement? Most likely, you are somewhere in between. We often think about money and happiness in the context of how we spend it, but happiness is at least partially a function of how we spend our hours, and we spend a big chunk of our hours earning money. One study, published in *Science* in 2004, measured working women's happiness through the day. The researchers found that, averaged for all of them, the morning commute, working, and the evening commute ranked as the bottom three events. Since we spend more hours working than chatting with friends on the phone or (if you have a full-time job) watching TV—activities that are higher up the hedonic list—if you find work that is as pleasant for you as social phone calls, it seems logical that you'll get quite a happiness boost.

2. **How would you like to use your money?** This is a bigger question than the usual task of creating a budget, because it requires pondering what matters to us and getting beyond our usual money mind-set—that is, that there's never enough. Just as many of us as-

sume we have no time, and so we never bother to figure out what we'd like to spend our hours doing, we often assume we can't afford X, Y, or Z, or that only rich people experience certain things and we'll never be rich. We assume certain expenditures are absolutely necessary, even though much of humanity survives without them. And so we live with a constrained mental picture of our lives.

Getting beyond this requires a somewhat different money journal, one focused not just on the numbers but on how they make you feel.

So keep your records of money coming in, and your receipts and bills for a day, a week, a month, or a year if you'd like. I originally wrote this paragraph on a Saturday night (a long story—but one indication that I'm in the right job), and my two main expenditures for that day beyond 1/30th of a rent payment were swim lessons for my kids and a trip to the grocery store. I felt good about the swim lessons. My kids learned some skills, and the instructor we hired off Craigslist was cheerful and encouraging, even if we did soon realize that progress would require a more relaxed environment than the apartment complex pool. On my grocery receipt, some items triggered more positive feelings than others. Sandwich bread and raisins are no one's idea of a good time. But I felt nearly giddy splurging on a big package of frozen king crab legs.

Over time, you can use these cues to hash out what you enjoy and value. You can deduce, to use economic terms, what has the highest utility function for you. The answers may be surprising, but they'll probably be enlightening, if you pay attention.

Looking at my day, I figured out that I was happy to pay for swim lessons for two reasons. One is that I hope to accumulate many hours splashing in pools or in the waves with my kids over the next few years. The other is that, especially in this economy, I like to support "soloists" like myself, particularly women, who are plying their trades on their own. That's an insight that has me rethinking how to conduct all kinds of business. As for the grocery store receipt, my husband loves king crab legs. Buying them was a little present for him, and as we'll discuss in the chapter on giving, research finds that spending money on other people is definitely correlated with happiness (even if the gift was, technically, from a joint checking account). Buying the crab legs also had me anticipating cooking a special meal with my husband. Anticipating enjoyable experiences is another key component of happiness.

As you look at your receipts and bills, and tease out what gives an expenditure a high utility function, start to write this down. Some of my winners include:

▶ Supporting small businesses and sole proprietors

▶ Eating well, particularly with good company, and particularly outside

▶ Gifts that delight people I love

▶ Flowers and plants

▶ Visiting distinctive places, from strawberry patches to Morocco

▶ Making music and listening to it (live)

▶ Books, magazines, notebooks, pens, and other ways of dressing up the printed word

What makes you happy when it comes to money? Write these categories down and keep them in your wallet, or wherever you pay bills. That way, you can remember, as you're debating where to eat, that supporting your local pizzeria owner is more in line with your values than swinging by a fast-food chain, and that spending money on a magazine subscription will make you happier than buying a new pair of pants.

THE $10,000 LIST

As you start to understand what gives you the most satisfaction, you can start to dream a little more about what your money can do. We all know the usual dreams: the house, the car, the 401(k), the college funds. What about the more creative ones? There are lots of ways to buy happiness. In the introduction, I asked what people would change about their lives if they had all the money in the world, or at least all they wanted. In this chapter, I'll bring it down to earth a little more. Say you got an unexpected (tax-free!) $50,000 inheritance. Responsible person that you are, you put the first $40,000 toward savings, retiring any debts you have, and your usual charitable commitments. But $10,000 can be fun money.

What would you do with it? The only ground rule is that, looking back on your life, you'd remember, fondly, the way you spent that 10 grand. You could:

▶ Fly to Mongolia ($2,000), then do the 11-day REI "Mongolia Multisport" trip, featuring camel trekking and sleeping in desert camps ($4,000, plus $900 single supplement), and tack on a few days of R&R and pricey souvenir shopping at the end.

▶ Commission a major choral work from an up-and-coming composer ($2,500), hire singers to perform it ($200 × 20 is $4,000), book a venue ($2,500) and spend another $1,000 promoting the premiere.

▶ Produce three episodes of short, dramatic works you've written for the Web, running about $1,000 per finished minute.

▶ Earn your pilot's license (up to $10,000 depending on the flight school). If you happen to find a bargain, you could use the rest of the $10,000 to rent a plane for several hours to test that license out.

▶ Publish a family history ($4,000 to self-publish a nice hardbound color book), with help from a genealogical researcher ($2,000) and a writer ($2,000) who'd craft vignettes based on family interviews to accompany the photos (add in another $2,000 to get new ones taken of everyone).

▶ Via DonorsChoose.org, a Web site that lets you sponsor projects in school classrooms, pay for 125 kids in Indianapolis to spend the day at the zoo ($10 each, or $1,250), and then repeat this gift for the next eight years.

▶ Get 80 one-hour massages ($100 per massage, plus a $25 tip), dispatching any tension into some alternate universe.

▶ Pay the salaries of six to seven library workers in rural Morocco ($1,500 each).

▶ Cruise around Alaska in an ocean-view suite with a grand piano ($9,500 for two people if you look for a deal), and then pay someone to serenade you with all your favorite jazz standards ($500 for a few hours—as long as the musician's already onboard).

▶ Use unpaid leave at work to take a one-month retreat somewhere—maybe to a grand estate on the ocean (let's say $5,000 for off-season rent)—where you work solely on projects you love, and pay your usual bills from the remainder (another $5,000 perhaps, though yours may vary).

▶ Buy top-of-the-line camping equipment ($3,000 for tents, sleeping bags, backpacks, and boots), fly your family to Yellowstone ($3,000 for five of you), and try it out for a week (with a $750 car rental so you can go deep into the park). Document the adventure on your new digital camera ($1,500 for a nice model with zoom lens for the wildlife), make photo books for reliving it ($200 or so), and spend the rest on nice meals and a hotel to recover from your outdoor adventure.

▶ Hire a babysitter and go out for a nice dinner plus dancing with your partner ($200 for the whole evening) every Friday night for a year.

▶ Via GlobalGiving.org, a Web site that lets you fund development projects around the world, send 250 children in the remote rural villages of Rajasthan, India, to school ($40 each).

▶ Start an award for new poetry ($1,000 per year for five years), and create and promote a Web site to feature the artists you discover (another $5,000 to do a really bang-up job).

Spend some time thinking through your list. Draw up real proposals. Ask your friends what they'd do. Vote on whose $10,000 ideas are the best. Are the answers practical? Who knows? But it's fun to think about exactly what $10,000 can enable—a first step in pondering, broadly, what kinds of choices we sometimes make without thinking about the opportunity costs. Because, just as a reference point, Chris Rice and his wife had a no-less-memorable wedding for about $10,000 below what the average couple spends these days. And now they get to ponder exactly what else that ring could buy.

GETTING

CHAPTER 2

Don't Scrimp More, Make More

In the decade since reality TV has come to dominate our airwaves, cable networks have come up with increasingly creative—some would say ridiculous—premises for new programs. I normally shy away from human train wrecks. I tried to watch *Jersey Shore* and had to stop. But even so, I can't get a few scenes from TLC's *Extreme Couponing* out of my head.

For the series pilot, which aired in January 2011, four coupon enthusiasts from various parts of the country took a camera crew shopping and explained their tricks. They all followed roughly the same methodology—match manufacturer coupons with store sales and stock up when you get a steal—but they all had their own quirks. Amanda Ostrowski of Cincinnati bought a $35,000 insurance policy for her two-room stockpile. Joanie Demer of McKinleyville, California, took her son and her pregnant friend Dumpster diving for discarded circulars in order to cut a $638.64 grocery bill down to $2.64. Joyce House, a retired nurse in Philadelphia, claimed not to have paid for toothpaste or deodorant in 34 years. And Nathan Engels of Villa Hills, Kentucky, invested in an industrial paper cutter for faster clipping. In the series pilot, he special-ordered 1,100 boxes of Total from his local grocery store after he realized he could get $4,000 worth for about $150.

For Engels, it was all a game, "like chess," he said in the show. "You're trying to beat the opponent, which is the store." He donated the Total to a food bank, thus playing Robin Hood with his coupons, which was certainly a creative way to help the needy in his community. But I don't think the reason the show is so popular, and why TLC ultimately extended the pilot into a series, is the potential for low-budget philanthropy. Rather, in these tight times, people are fascinated by coupons because they represent a certain thrifty mind-set, which has been celebrated since Ben Franklin told us that a penny saved is a penny earned. Because we shop at the grocery store more often than other places, that's where we think we should put this thrift into practice. Many of us pride ourselves on our ability to stretch a dollar, even if by objective standards we don't need to. According to statistics from Nielsen, coupon "enthusiasts" (very heavy users) are more likely to be from households earning over $100,000 per year than under $30,000. There's a story called "Ode to His Frugal Wife" in Thomas Stanley and William Danko's bestselling book, *The Millionaire Next Door*, in which a man gives his wife $8 million worth of stock in a company he recently took public. "She smiled," the authors write, "never changing her position at the kitchen table, where she continued to cut out twenty-five- and fifty-cents-off food coupons from the week's supply of newspapers"—either not realizing or not caring that an $8 million stock portfolio goes up and down $8,000 in the time it takes to save $8 via the coupon route.

Nathan Engels notwithstanding, this dollar-stretching mind-set often has a pink cast to it. We pay homage to the belief, as Betty Friedan described it in *The Feminine Mystique*, that "Women can save more money by their managerial talents inside the home than they can bring into it by outside work."

How often this gospel of thrift is true in practice is an open question. Ostrowski works full-time as a storage facility manager yet told the *Extreme Couponing* producers that she devoted 70 hours a week to her coupon habit. I'm always skeptical of 70-hour workweek claims, but if this is true, in 70 hours she cut her $1,175.33 bill down to $51.67, after paying $70 to a clipping service. So that's $1,053.66 in savings. If that was one week's haul, she'd net about $15 an hour. That's decent, and if she's overestimating her coupon time, the rate per hour comes out much better. However, since a normal two-person household with no children would never have bought four figures' worth of groceries for one week, it's not clear how much she's "saving."

Still, thrift, as defined by trimming your spending, is widely considered a virtue, and whenever someone needs more cash in her life, this is the standard advice: look at the money going out, particularly for food and clothes, or little luxuries like having the dry cleaner iron your shirts, and figure out where you can scale back.

In other words, play defense.

What seldom gets mentioned, though, is that there's another option: offense. You can try to earn more, too.

I know why this isn't the standard advice. People understand how to cut their Netflix subscriptions or cut coupons, even if they don't do it on the scale of Ostrowski, Engels, et al. Corporations suffer from this same single-mindedness. Whenever the economy drifts south, companies inflict major rounds of cost cutting, slicing research budgets, charging employees for coffee, or—worse—showing them the door. Figuring out a way to bring more in when, unlike a government, you can't tax, is less straightforward and taps into a few deeply held, if misguided, beliefs about money. But in this chapter I'll argue that changing one's income, within a range, is certainly doable. Done right, it's also much more pleasant than cutting life's small pleasures—say, your favorite brand of yogurt, even if you don't have a coupon—and the upside is far greater than what most people could save at the grocery store. It is the difference between a 50-cent coupon and a $5,000 raise. Thrift is a virtue, but if the definition of thrift is "wise economy in the management of money," why can't we expand that concept to include obtaining more money to manage in the first place? Aiming to make more may not get you all the money in the world, but it will at least bring you closer to the amount you'd like than you'll get by not paying for deodorant.

MORE MONEY = MORE HAPPINESS?

The subtitle of this book promises to share with you what the happiest people know about getting and spending. For the rest of the chapters to make sense, you must accept that the matters of money and happiness are related. To me, this seems logical. Stripped of the emotions and drama surrounding it, money is nothing more than a means to acquire the goods and services you've deemed worth acquiring. Naturally, the more money you have, the more able you are to acquire these things. The upside with money—unlike other resources, such as time—is that it is generally possible to increase the amount you have. Even the mightiest among us is granted no more than 168 hours a week. But unless you live in some authoritarian and centrally planned economy where you are shackled to your current circumstances, you can probably find some way to increase your income. The question is, what impact could that have on your life?

Often, a very positive one. In 2010, psychologist Daniel Kahneman and economist Angus Deaton released a paper in the *Proceedings of the National Academy of Sciences* evaluating people's emotional well-being (day-to-day feelings) and overall life satisfaction (how people feel their lives are going) based on income. Crunching data from Gallup's surveys of more than 450,000 U.S. residents, they found

that "the effects of income on individuals' life evaluations show no sa-
tiation, at least to an amount well over $120,000." The charts accom-
panying the paper show the life satisfaction line continuing to rise
past $160,000 in household income, above which a random Gallup
sample just would not include much more data.

Day-to-day emotional state was a slightly different matter. As one
might imagine, low income was not a recipe for happiness. "Lack of
money brings both emotional misery and low life evaluation," the authors write, and is also inclined to make people feel angry. These measures all got better up to a household income of $75,000 a year, then
leveled out. "Beyond $75,000 in the contemporary United States . . .
higher income is neither the road to experienced happiness nor the road
to the relief of unhappiness or stress, although higher income continues
to improve individuals' life evaluations," Kahneman and Deaton write.

Why the split on these different measures? Happiness is complicated, and day-to-day emotional state is influenced by many things—
one's innate temperament, for instance, and the traffic on the way to
work. Seventy-five thousand dollars may be the point where you have
enough money to solve minor irritations, or stave off the big woes that
really affect happiness. You laugh off a burned dinner and call for
pizza. An unexpectedly large car repair bill doesn't mean you can't
pay your mortgage. You probably have health insurance and, more
likely than people with less money, better health. But beyond that,
more money—at least to the point where the data becomes less
available—doesn't help much. In the United States at least, $100,000
or $120,000 means you're still riding the train at rush hour rather
than being helicoptered onto the roof of your office building. Six figures, though significant, are not enough for most people to completely
stop worrying about their finances, or to immediately have enough
wealth that they work only because they want to. Work stress can also
affect day-to-day happiness, and one could presume that people earning, say, $1 million per year might have some work stress in their lives.

Nonetheless, $75,000 is more than the median American household income. This study implies that many people could boost their day-to-day mood by earning more money, and that the vast majority of us would think our lives were going better, overall, as our household income climbed. So I'm a bit baffled as to why we tell ourselves that money can't buy happiness. It is certainly possible to find tales of wealthy people who are miserable and think their lives are a total waste, but in a world of 7 billion people it is possible to find anecdotes regarding just about anything. As I've been probing the relationship between money and happiness, I've realized we champion a lot of these beliefs about income out of some perceived sense of morality, rather than any particular logic. In the Bible, 1 Timothy 6:10 states that "the love of money is the root of all evil," which we often shorten, tellingly, to "money is the root of all evil."

There are problems with these beliefs, though. For starters, few of us, if offered a $10,000 raise, would decline for fear of our souls. And what does it mean to be rich, anyway? Even the most saintly among us seldom decide to move to, say, rural India and live on $1 a day. If it is truly easier for a camel to go through the eye of a needle than for a rich man to enter the kingdom of heaven, then we are all in trouble, since modern inhabitants of the developed world are among the richest people in human history—far more comfortable than those who'd achieved great comfort in the Roman Empire of Saint Paul's day. And so, hopefully, we can read the Bible verse in context. The love of money is the root of all evil, Paul writes, because "in pursuit of it some have wandered from the faith and spiked themselves on many a painful thorn." This implies that money itself is not necessarily the problem—the fault lies in refusing to put God before money. But earning more doesn't mean a person will worship money, and earning less doesn't mean the person will be immune from such temptations. Other things can become idols, too. Debt can quickly become a master. A lack of savings may force someone to stay in a job that compromises his morals. Having money, on the other hand, gives you the means to act on good intentions. The Good Samaritan didn't just stop to help the wounded man by the roadside. He paid for his room, board, and upkeep until he recovered.

Another misguided belief about money is that as we earn more we just spend more, therefore thwarting any attempts to get ahead. This has an element of truth to it. Richer people do like to spend more on cars, for instance. A few years ago, *Forbes* magazine crunched some numbers for its Web site on income and consumption and found that the poorest 20 percent of American households spent 14.7 percent of their overall expenditures on transportation, and the richest spent 17.4 percent, a higher amount both in percentage and in dollar terms—and a phenomenon I can't say I entirely understand. But overall, people don't spend all the extra money. A 2009 CareerBuilder.com survey found that about 61 percent of workers, overall, were living paycheck to paycheck, but only about 30 percent of those earning over $100,000 were. That's still a shockingly high percentage, to be sure, but a lot less high. The Federal Reserve conducts surveys every three years to track consumer finances by income percentile. The Fed reports that higher-income families are more likely to save:

INCOME PERCENTILE	PERCENT OF FAMILIES WHO SAVE
40th–60th	57.8%
60th–80th	66.8%
80th–90th	72.9%
90th+	84.8%

Since saving and investing small amounts will produce less wealth over time than compound interest calculators seem to indicate (as I'll discuss in the upcoming retirement chapter), amassing large amounts of wealth really requires saving and investing large amounts to begin with. While a surprisingly high number of upper-income families don't do this—we can all ponder what is going on with the 15.2 percent of families in the top 10 percent of the income distribution who *don't* save—it is easier for them than for those with less.

This is pretty obvious arithmetic, so it's worth asking why most personal finance literature advocates scrimping more (playing defense) instead of earning more (playing offense) as the best way to get ahead. I assume this is because most of us believe, as *The Millionaire Next Door* puts it, that "the majority of people do not have the ability to increase their incomes substantially." Thus, the financial advice we find most pertinent shows how to divvy up our certain-sized pie, investing a slice in the hopes of getting long-term compound returns. We assume there is no way to make our pie bigger.

But is this true? In a broad and long-term sense, household income clearly involves a big element of choice, particularly among people with a reasonable amount of education.

Our occupation is the first important variable. Often, jobs that involve broadly similar skill levels and the same number of years of schooling pay vastly different amounts. Scrolling through the Bureau of Labor Statistics' National Occupational Employment and Wage Estimates spreadsheets on median/mean wages for different jobs reveals just that.

Take the field of engineering. All engineering fields are highly paid, but some are significantly higher paying than others:

TYPE OF ENGINEERING	MEAN ANNUAL WAGE
Industrial	$77,090
Mechanical	$80,580
Civil	$81,180
Biomedical	$82,550
Electrical	$86,250

TYPE OF ENGINEERING	MEAN ANNUAL WAGE
Chemical	$91,670
Aerospace	$96,270
Petroleum	$119,960

If you look on the lower end of the architectural and engineering occupations, there are differences, too. Electrical drafters earn $54,800 per year. Mechanical drafters earn $49,790. An extra $5,000 per year, or a bit over $400 a month, isn't a huge amount if you prefer one kind of drafting to the other. But if you're neutral as a student in these disciplines, $400 a month (even after you take out taxes) is more than most people will save with coupons.

Or perhaps you're a creative type with an interest in design. There are wide differences here, too:

TYPE OF DESIGN	MEAN ANNUAL WAGE
Floral	$24,940
Graphic	$47,820
Set & Exhibits	$50,600
Interior	$51,990
Fashion	$74,410

The BLS data produces some surprises in terms of perceived pecking order. Many writers and editors tell themselves they'd earn more in public relations, but this isn't always true. Editors bank $58,440. Public relations specialists take in $59,370. Writers and authors earn $64,560 per year, though admittedly this figure hides a huge variance, given that it puts John Grisham and me in the same category. I always assumed that medical assistants made more than dental assistants, but dental assistants make $34,000 and medical assistants make $29,450. Legal secretaries make much more than medical secretaries ($42,940 vs. $31,450). GED/adult literacy teachers make vastly more than preschool teachers ($50,390 vs. $27,450). This is likely because more adult ed instructors are licensed teachers working for large school districts, but if you do have a teaching license and are looking to transition into something outside K–12, there are massive financial consequences when deciding to go one way or the other.

Even on the lower ends of the salary scale, specialties matter. Logging equipment operators make $32,870, and agricultural equipment operators make $25,220. Tree trimmers make more than groundskeepers. Small differences in occupation matter on the high end, too. While astronomers make $102,740, atmospheric and space scientists make $85,160. Geoscientists ($92,710) outearn hydrologists ($76,760), and internists ($183,990) outearn family practitioners ($168,550).

Now, granted, this may be fascinating and useful if you are 20 years old and pondering what to do with your life. It is slightly less useful if you are deep enough into your career that switching occupations would be difficult or would involve too many years of training (like going to medical school at age 45) to get a payoff. But if you are looking to change careers, and give yourself a two-year horizon, there are definitely lucrative options. In February 2011, Louise Tutelian wrote a piece for CBS's MoneyWatch.com on high-paying in-demand careers that required less than two years of training:

▸ mobile applications developers

▸ global supply chain managers

▸ financial advisors

▸ online marketing directors

▸ financial analysts for the gaming industry

▶ sales managers for medical equipment

▶ radiation therapists

▶ business development managers in solar energy

The caveat is that these kinds of lists change all the time. Buggy whip factory managers may have been in high demand once, too. It's seldom worth going into a job you don't like just to earn more, and I can't say that any of the jobs on Tutelian's list appeal to me. But if you don't like your current job, then it's always possible you'd like a better-paying one more. Why not spend the time you might be cutting coupons pondering that question—or taking a class—instead?

The second important variable in household income is how many household members participate in the paid labor force. Households in the top income quintile have an average of about two income earners per family, whereas households in the middle have fewer. Sometimes this is because there simply aren't two adults in the household, and sometimes it's because one party is caring for children or pursuing other projects. Taking time out of the workforce obviously has financial consequences, and not just for the years when one stays home. Economist Sylvia Ann Hewlett's research on "off-ramping" finds that women who take three or more years out of the workforce earn just 63 percent of the salary, upon return, of people who stay in.

A third variable? How many hours those income earners work per week. A variety of surveys, including some from the Pew Research Center, have found that the majority of moms wish to work part-time. Usually this is for what we think of as work-life balance reasons. I've argued that, since there are 168 hours in a week, working 40 hours for pay seems more balanced to me than working 20. But even if there are work-life balance benefits, there are definitely financial downsides. Warren Farrell, author of *Why Men Earn More*, crunched census numbers and found that people who worked 45 hours per week earn more than double the income of those who work 34 hours a week, even though they're working only about a third more. The income cut is more pronounced as you go down to the 19 hours per week the American Time Use Survey finds the average mom who works part-time puts in. Scaling up from part-time to full-time can make a big difference in household income, as can taking on overtime hours, if that's feasible in your job.

Of course, when I suggest scaling up the total number of hours worked per household, people often claim that child-care costs will eat up any additional dollars earned. This can be true, though it doesn't have to be, particularly if the children are older. Some creative couples have even figured out ways to keep child-care costs down with young kids and two full-time workers. Joy Charde and her husband, for instance, have two children ages two and under. Her husband, a computer programmer for New York State, works from 7 A.M. to 3 P.M. Joy, the business manager of their local library, works from 4 P.M. to 8 P.M., plus three hours at home at that job (plus blogging at CreativeMamma.com), usually when at least one kid is asleep. That way, they both put in 35- to 40-hour weeks, without springing for day care. That obviously wouldn't work for all families, but not all work must be done from 9 A.M. to 5 P.M. in a certain location, either.

A final factor in household income is how aggressive people are about seeking out higher compensation, even within the same jobs. According to Linda Babcock and Sara Laschever's 2003 book, *Women Don't Ask*, young men are four times more likely to negotiate their first salary than young women, resulting in $500,000 more in earnings by age 60. Time spent figuring out how to trim household expenses could also be spent practicing negotiating techniques or flushing out a higher-paying job offer, thus inducing a current employer to match it. It could be spent building up a portfolio to make the case for that next promotion, which comes with a high enough salary that paying $4 for a tube of toothpaste every two months doesn't seem like a big deal.

THE 1099 MIND-SET

So that's the long run. Even in the short run, though, I think income is malleable. The belief that it isn't results from what I call a "W-2" mind-set. Shortly after the new year, anybody who receives a regular paycheck in the United States gets a nice, compartmentalized statement called a W-2 showing exactly how much she earned during the previous year. If you work for wages or salary at one job, this number is pretty much set at whatever you and your employer have negotiated, and will not change unless you change jobs or get a raise—shifts that don't happen all that often.

But a sizable number of American workers are "1099-ers"—freelancers, temporary workers, or self-employed individuals who are paid on a project basis, thus making their income vary quite a bit from month to month. If work is scarce, income goes down, but when it's abundant, one can make a tidy sum in a relatively short time.

Getting some, or even all, of your income this way changes how you think about what you make. When you see how closely the amount of work you do is tied to income, you realize how extra effort can be converted into extra money.

Here's a question to ask yourself: would you be able to come up with an extra $2,000 in 30 days? This is a question economists sometimes ask to figure out how many families are financially fragile, and one paper published by the National Bureau of Economic Research in May 2011 found that only half of Americans would definitely or probably be able to. Such statistics are usually cited to show Americans' low savings rate, but pulling money out of savings (or selling possessions or taking out a loan) isn't the only way to meet a sudden high expense. JP and Camille Noe Pagán of Ann Arbor, Michigan, know what they'd do to cover a $2,000 gap. Both are in the media industry and freelance full-time. The fact that neither of these parents of two small children draws a regular paycheck sounds risky—"there are still times in the middle of the night when I'm thinking this is totally insane," Camille says—but there are upsides. Specifically financial upsides. Because "the ability to hustle for clients and reposition is always there," Camille says, "I'm still making so much more than I would at a [salaried] job." She and JP have some regular assignments and both, through those, aim to make at least $4,000 a month, combined, to cover their usual bills. Camille generally hits closer to $5,000–$6,000 a month. One month, she set a goal to earn $10,000 and hit it, though it did require concerted efforts and working her network. She pitched new story ideas and told all the editors she knew, "I'm available." Because she'd built this network over time, many of them came through with assignments.

Earning $4,000 a month vs. $10,000 a month is a very different matter, and some families would find it difficult to plan spending, given that their household income could be somewhere around $48,000 (both parties earning the bare minimum), $72,000 (both earning $3,000 a month), $100,000 (one earning $3,000 a month, and the other hitting $5,000–$6,000), $144,000 (both of them consistently hitting $6,000 a month) or even closer to $200,000 (if they kept aiming for $10,000 a month). The Pagáns save in good times, banking 20 percent of their income and setting aside 25 percent for taxes. They keep their base expenses low, so they can pay their bills out of current cash flow even in rough months. What they lose in ability to plan spending, though, they make up for in the peace of mind that comes from knowing how they'd get more cash if they needed it.

For instance, when I first interviewed Camille in late 2010, she was expecting her second child. The family has health insurance, but their maternity coverage wasn't great. For a normal delivery, they figured they'd be on the hook for about $4,000, which they saved for. Complications, though, could get them a $20,000 bill. Covering that expense out of savings would have left them with much less of a cushion, and replenishing their savings would have been tough to do just by cutting coupons. But since both of them know how to "dial it up when I need to," as Camille put it, they felt pretty confident they could have rebuilt their savings within a few months to a year of working more intensely after she went back to work (and fortunately, baby Xavier was born healthy and on the cheap).

All-1099 families are rare, but they're not as rare as they used to be. And with 26 percent of the U.S. workforce identifying themselves as free agents, according to a 2009 Kelly Services survey, it appears many of us draw income apart from or in addition to a regular salary. The culture of moonlighting, always with us, has taken hold with a vengeance during the Great Recession. Working a second job conjures up images of reporting to a second work site after a long day at the first, but it can also be something more flexible or creative or fulfilling, and possibly even an opportunity to explore a new career path if you're successful. Various technological and sociological realities are converging these days to make sidelines more efficient and fun.

Take, for instance, the rise of Etsy and other online craft portals. Hobbyists have long cranked out wooden toys and homemade doll clothes in their garages, but that used to be where their creations stayed, unless the crafty person was particularly entrepreneurial and either opened a store (which takes capital), sold her goods at Christmas markets (which is seasonal at best), or, after 1997 or so, opened her own e-commerce site (which takes IT skills, though eBay definitely started making e-commerce easier for the non-technically inclined). These days, however, creative types have the option of uploading pictures into a craft portal's system, and using the portal's technology to connect with buyers for these niche products world-wide. It's proved to be quite a market, with Etsy sales rising from $88 million in 2008 to $181 million in 2009 to $314 million in 2010. The average seller doesn't necessarily make much; $314 million in sales divided by 400,000 sellers is just $785 per seller per year, but there are no barriers to entry. People with a lot of creative talent could do better.

Of course, selling crafts online is far from the only or most lucrative way to moonlight. A more straightforward way to boost your income is to freelance by doing whatever parts of your day job you actually like. If you're a teacher, you could tutor after school or on weekends, or teach online classes at night after your kids go to bed. If you're an editor, you can proofread cover letters, resumes, and school application essays. Tech folks can do freelance Web site work. Back when I was a 22-year-old intern at *USA Today*, I stretched my $1,200 monthly take-home pay by writing for other magazines, newspapers, and Web sites. I didn't earn much at first, but if you set your budget based on $1,200, an extra $500–$1,000 a month is a big win. I was able to bank almost all of it after taxes.

Various creative gigs—organizing, decorating, design—are also options. I used to think making money blogging was unlikely, but in the past year I've learned more about the finances of it and have found several people making reasonable money this way (including me, through a stint with BNET, which is part of CBS Interactive). Interestingly, some of the people who are most successfully boosting household income through their Web sites are money bloggers—whose sites are often filled with advice on how to trim expenses and cut back! I like the irony of this, though many of the best are quite upfront about it. They are savvy businesspeople, and in a tight economy, Web traffic flows quickly to sites offering coupons and deals.

Carrie Rocha of Minneapolis runs a blog called Pocket Your Dollars. She started it as a sideline while she was working full-time as the chief operating officer for a company (her husband had been going to school and caring for their two young daughters). She worked on it after 8 P.M. and in the mornings, and started making some money from it. But as her family's primary breadwinner, she was really glad she had the blog when she was laid off in early 2010. She could throw herself fully into the project, and by the end of the year it was getting 230,000 visits a month and grossing between $4,000 and $8,000 per month in ads and a similar amount in affiliate income. "The blog supports our family," she says—which is why she devotes plenty of her time toward growing the business.

Likewise, Kelly Whalen, the proprietor of The Centsible Life blog, reports that her site has increased her family's income by 50 percent. Whalen had long stayed home with her four kids, resulting in fairly tight finances—which has let her blog with authority on such topics as asking friends for diapers rather than toys or clothes for new babies. But now that she's bringing in a serious paycheck, "we're not as stressed out about every single penny," she says. She's found the time by cutting out other things, such as TV. Her youngest child will soon be in school. But even so, she's learned that "even if you have two hours of nap time you can do something with that. Any little extra bit helps."

Both these bloggers had to learn to be entrepreneurs on the job, and this is a skill set many of us don't come by naturally. I suspect that's the reason many people looking for sidelines or even full-time entrepreneurial ventures get caught up in multilevel marketing schemes, or click on online banner ads touting claims like "Mom earns $9,000 a month working part-time at home!" With these ventures, someone has at least done the basic work of figuring out a business for you, even if the business models almost never pay off for people other than those at the top.

Other times, people go for obvious sidelines, such as becoming landlords, because there are whole bookshelves on the topic. It can be great work if you're suited for it. Elizabeth Simmerman and her husband supplement their finances (both are consultants) with income from a rental property in the Boston area. They have enjoyed the experience. But "there are a lot of upfront costs," she reports, and there's nothing fun after a 60-hour workweek about "killing a weekend because you have to replace the ceiling." Not everyone likes repair work (or paying other people to do repair work), and there are risks to this business as in any other, as people who bought "investment" properties in Las Vegas in 2007 soon discovered.

Some people, unsure how to market themselves, seek out work that is extremely low paying but requires no specialized skills, like filling out surveys online. Trust me, your time is worth more than the few cents you'll get by clicking boxes.

A better option is to train yourself to think like an entrepreneur. Broadly, you do this by asking three questions:

1. **What skills do I have or can I learn that I enjoy using?** "There are plenty of basic life skills you may already have," says Whalen, such as playing an instrument, speaking another language, doing calligraphy, proofreading, writing resumes, and so forth.

2. **Which of these skills will people pay me to use?** Don't assume that there's no market if you think creatively. Even sitting around reading or watching TV can be a "skill" in the context of being around to receive packages at houses where there's no one home during the workday or during a scheduled weekend delivery. Make a long list.

3. **How can I find these people?** In the above example, your best bet might be to contract with a concierge service that pinch-hits for executives called away for last-minute business trips during times when three plumbers were sup-

posed to show up to give estimates. Ask around. Pay attention. That's what entrepreneurs do, and if you start thinking this way, you're bound to come up with some way of making a little extra on the side, or potentially finding something you'd like to try as a full-time gig.

HOW CAN I AFFORD IT?

To be sure, not everyone can change her income and not everyone wants to. But sometimes the simple act of looking at something in a different way can make a big impact. Take the subject of time. Rather than say "I don't have time," when you feel crunched, you can say "it's not a priority" and see how that feels. Often, this is a perfectly adequate explanation for why you're not choosing to spend your time doing something, like dusting your blinds. These words remind us that time is a choice.

The same concept applies to money. Rather than say "I can't afford it," as long as "it" is within reason, what if you started asking yourself "*How* can I afford it?" Kelly Whalen, the Centsible Life blogger, made a life list of experiences and possessions she wanted to have. One item on that list was to take her family—all four kids—to Disney World. There are lots of different ways to do this. You can fly first class, stay in the nicest hotel you can find, and eat at the most expensive restaurants. What she opted to do was seize an opportunity: when one of her sons was attending a robotics competition there, she brought the rest of the family along. They hunted for deals and put a deposit on a hotel room in advance. She managed to get a free car rental from one of her blog sponsors (they had to drive from Philadelphia to transport the robots). They cut back on other expenses and, of course, her blog money made the trip more feasible than it would have been with only one income in her family.

Research prices and figure out how you might bring in enough cash to cover the various choices that appeal most to you. If you want to take two months off between jobs, figure out how much cash it would take to cover your bills, and how many additional hours you'd need to work, or how you might moonlight temporarily to hit that. If you can figure out a way to afford it, the only other question you need to ask yourself is whether you want to.

But many of us never even get to the first question—the how part—which is too bad. When you know you can most likely bring in more money through a series of steps such as calling another editor or calling your clients and saying you're running a special, you don't necessarily need to think in terms of cutting back first. You can see if the same investment of time will let you make more than you'd save by scrimping.

That's a game-changing concept. Most money books and financial gurus would tell you the opposite, that you should pinch every penny and cut every little luxury in order to afford the big things in life—a house, a cozy retirement, or a family. I'll argue in the later chapters that we might actually be just as content spending less on big-ticket items, which would leave more room for the little things that bring us joy. This book is about how to buy happiness. Consider the latte, that first small indulgence people think to rip from their budgets when they need more cash. What a nice, creamy kick to start a cold morning. You can try to make it at home, but as the owner of a coffeemaker that allegedly froths milk, I can attest it is not the same. Missing your coffee can make you grumpy all day, and I'll bet your co-workers and family members would be grateful if you spent a few extra bucks on making yourself tolerable to be around. In the same way, sometimes it's nice to walk into the grocery store and simply buy whatever you'd like to eat, like king crab legs, whether they're on sale or not. They're cheaper than a seafood dinner in a restaurant! Not that there's anything wrong with spending money in restaurants either. Going out to eat is a great way to celebrate birthdays or friends visiting from out of town. Even the office lunch can be a way to nurture relationship capital at work—doable in theory with brown bagging, particularly if your boss is modeling this behavior, but sometimes harder to pull off. Food and entertainment expenses may be easy to trim, but the hours we spend eating, doing leisure activities, and socializing are often the most pleasant of our days.

That's a problem for the scrimping mind-set because, to add insult to injury, not only is lowering the guillotine on these little luxuries unpleasant, it doesn't free up as much money in most families' budgets as you'd imagine, given the pain you're inflicting. The average household spends 7.6 percent of its budget on food consumed at home and 5.3 percent on food eaten out. Even if you got rid of all eating out and cut your grocery budget in half, you'd free up 9.1 percent of the average income, or a little over $4,500 on $50,000. Since upper-income households spend a lower percentage of their income on food than middle-income families, these households would save proportionally less (figure $7,000 or so on $100,000). This isn't nothing, and if your bills were much higher to start with, because you've never even figured out how to turn on your stove, you could save more. But it would still take years to make progress toward a 20 percent house down payment or a solid rainy day fund simply by cutting these variable expenditures. And—most important—you'd be perpetually ticked off all those years, because you'd be subsisting on rice and beans and never going out to eat.

This is a microcosm of a broader economic truth. Over the past few years as the economy cratered, headlines have been full of stories about corporate cost cutting. People have renegotiated vendor contracts until there's nothing left to squeeze. Some corporate cafeterias have even attacked the salad bars. But when you're facing tough times, getting rid of the mesclun mix won't do much except make your employees miserable. A better option? Do what the best-managed companies do and invest in things that will grow revenue in the future.

Dave Lassman, vice president of operations at Leed's, a Pittsburgh-area company that makes promotional products (such as conference swag) reports that this is exactly what his firm did during the recent recession. "We looked at our market, at our competitors, and said we have some opportunity to take some market share," he says. So they hired people in product development while everyone else was doing layoffs. As a result, during the recovery, sales have been "higher than we expected and more than the industry average."

Could you do the same? How hard would it be to increase your income by 12 percent? This would produce the after-tax equivalent of that 9.1 percent you might save through extreme couponing or an all-ramen-noodle diet. If you like your job and figure out a way to do more of it, or you figure out a sideline that you enjoy, this could be a lot more pleasant than Dumpster diving for coupon circulars. If you could boost your income by more than 12 percent, you could start setting serious money aside for long-term priorities without giving up today's little pleasures. Saving is hard when it requires cutting back from your current standard of living with daily doses of deprivation. It's less hard when it's gravy money. Maybe none of this is doable, but it's worth pondering.

I have struggled to think this way myself. I grew up in a coupon-clipping household, albeit not one given to stockpiles, paper cutters, or bulk circulars. We had more modest ambitions. Still, I think of the grocery store as a place to try to save money, and that saving money in the grocery store is what I should be doing as a thrifty home economist who does her own highlights rather than going to the salon. I think this way even though I recognize that the nights I'm most likely to order pizza are the nights when there are no groceries I want to eat in the house. It takes a lot of coupons to atone for a $17 pizza.

Over the past few years, though, I have tried to change my

scrimping mind-set by cultivating a few markets that I don't write for often but which will take a lot of what I suggest. Anytime I catch myself eyeing a $1-off-fruit-cups coupon in the SmartSource circular that comes with the *Wall Street Journal* (an odd pairing, if you think about it), I go send an e-mail to an editor. It doesn't always work, but it often does.

Of course, this raises a question: if I know I can earn more money by working more or harder, at least up to a point of diminishing returns, why don't I? This gets at the broader issue of income being a choice, to the second part of the "how can I afford it?" question: do I want to? The Pagáns might be able to earn $200,000 a year if they slammed on the gas, but they often don't aim for that, because there are always competing priorities.

One is a more relaxed lifestyle. I find my work pretty enjoyable and more relaxing than watching a movie, but I'm probably in the minority on this one. Linda Formichelli, host of the blog The Renegade Writer, tells me that for a few years, she kept spending more and would then tell herself, "Now I have to earn more to cover it!" She added expenses to her budget such as personal training, an outside rent-by-the-hour office, and cable TV ("just to watch *Project Runway*, but didn't I deserve it after working that hard?"). And she did earn it without working too many hours, coming up with e-books, courses, new article ideas, coaching clients, and so forth.

The problem was that she really didn't enjoy the hustle. "One day I was so stressed that my stomach hurt so much that I literally couldn't get out of my chair," she tells me. "I had an appointment with my life coach later that day, and she said, 'You know, Linda, every time we have a session you want me to help you find new challenges, new projects, and more ways to make money. But I can see it's stressing you out. Have you ever thought of cutting down instead?'" So she did.

While income is correlated with happiness, more income is not the only thing that makes people happy. Some projects make us happier than others, and sometimes work is an investment. We opt for lower-paying work we enjoy that could have an upside, even if it's only a psychic one, vs. more immediately remunerative work that doesn't. That's one reason I haven't ghostwritten a book in three years.

Jaime Tardy and her family made a similar decision. I found Jaime because she writes a blog called Eventual Millionaire, in which she interviews a different millionaire every week and talks about how her family climbed out of $70,000 in debt in a short time. But what I find just as interesting about her is that she and her husband consciously chose to cut their income by half in pursuit of happiness.

She had been earning about $100,000 a year in the corporate world, frequently jetting off to different locations. Her husband is a performer, doing shows that feature contortion, fire-eating, juggling, and so on. He had been earning around $40,000 a year and was also on the road a lot. Since she was earning more than two thirds of the family income, the obvious solution, when they had a baby and didn't want to deal with the logistics of having both parents traveling, was that he would scale down and stay local. The problem was that "I always hated my job," Jaime says. Whereas he "absolutely loves what he does." If she worked more and he worked less, they'd both be miserable.

So they agreed on a different solution. He is working to scale up his career—plotting ways that he can charge more for shows and seek out new venues—and she launched a business coaching entrepreneurs. She earns much less than before but has also limited her work hours and knows that she could work more if she needed or wanted to. For the moment she doesn't, because the Tardy family completely changed their expense structure, moving to a house in a much cheaper state. In the future, though, maybe they will decide to change their income again. "I know we can make $140,000 a year," Jaime says. But this time, "I'll get to do it myself," in her own way, and doing what she loves. With both family members enjoying their work, they're feeling pretty content—which is the point of this book on money and happiness, regardless of the numbers on one's tax return.

CHAPTER 3

Rethink Retirement

Judith Van Ginkel is 72 years old and works 50–60 hours a week. But despite this grueling schedule, she calls herself "the luckiest person I know."

Here's the reason for her happiness: Van Ginkel, who has worked in the health field since 1981, spends her days running Every Child Succeeds, a home visitation program she started with the United Way of Greater Cincinnati and Cincinnati Children's Hospital. Over the past decade, the social workers on her team have checked in more than 370,000 times on 17,000 at-risk pregnant women and their children, ensuring that these growing families get proper medical care and support. They screen for maternal depression and offer suggestions on reading and playing with kids. They teach nutrition and monitor babies' growth and development. As a result of their vigilance, the infant mortality rate among participant families clocks in at 4.7 per 1,000 births, below the national average of 6.8 per 1,000, despite these families' poverty rates—an outcome that Van Ginkel is justly proud of. "I'm going to continue doing this as long as I can do it well," she says. She leaves the house at 7:15 A.M. and "tries" to get home by 6 or 6:30 P.M. She takes time off to travel with her husband, but otherwise, the way she is spending her golden years—down to the full-time paycheck she's earning—looks nothing like the "Ah, retirement . . . Golf yesterday, golf today, golf tomorrow" sentiment I saw displayed on a pillow recently.

Van Ginkel is more energetic than most, but she's not the only senior who's firmly attached to the workforce. According to the Bureau of Labor Statistics, after decades of decline, the employment of workers aged 65 and over increased 101 percent between 1977 and 2007, compared with an overall labor force expansion of 59 percent. This brought the labor force participation rate among people over age 65 up to 16.8 percent in 2008, which sounds low but includes people who are right up to death's door. Among younger seniors (those aged 65 to 69) a full 30.7 percent are working or looking for work. The BLS predicts this figure will rise to 36.9 percent by 2018, since surveys of baby boomers find that many who are still working don't intend to retire as soon as they're eligible for Social Security either.

Certainly, not all older workers feel as lucky about their situations as Van Ginkel, who is working largely because she wants to. But while economic woes have trapped some people in the workforce, the trend began during good times, and I think it is a positive development when we look at the intersection of money and happiness. It is a recognition that people both need and want to be part of the workforce longer in an era of longer lives. One study published in the *Journal of Occupational Health Psychology* in 2009 found that, controlling for initial health, people who kept working past retirement age in any field had fewer diseases and functional limitations, and those who kept working in the same field as they had before had better mental health outcomes. Seniors with solid incomes feel more secure, spend more, and invest their expertise in organizations in a way that boosts the economy—which helps younger workers, too.

Indeed, I believe the whole notion of retirement as we usually talk about it—that the money you save by brown-bagging lunches can and should finance two decades of golf in Florida—needs rethinking. Yes, you should save for your later years, and nothing in the next few pages should be construed as an invitation to raid your 401(k). Personally, I think people should save far more than they legally can in tax-advantaged retirement accounts, and far more than most people would consider a prudent rainy day fund. As the millions of Americans who have now been out of work for six months or more have discovered, economic pain can last for a long time. But I also believe that the retirement concept as the financial planning industry talks about it has been entirely oversold, given both the math and what work can be.

There are more compelling reasons to build up wealth than simply to enable you not to work for the last 20 to 30 years of your life. In terms of optimizing well-being, there are also more productive questions to ask yourself than how long you need to work before you can quit earning an income. Instead, what if we stopped thinking of work as a way to earn happiness in later years? What if we viewed work as a source of happiness now? What if, instead of figuring out when you'd have enough capital to retire, you spent that same energy finding a calling that you liked so much you didn't want to stop doing it? The happiest people build up wealth, sure. But, like Van Ginkel, they also know that meaningful work can be pleasurable in its own right, rather than a means to pleasure in the distant future.

FUZZY RETIREMENT MATH

Popular culture in the United States has long mirrored the experiences of the post–World War II baby boom. And so, sometime around the late 1980s when the people in this generational bulge realized they'd be turning 65 in the next few decades, we saw a corresponding boom in retirement literature. As a young intern at *Fortune* during the summer of 2000, I helped research a package in which we matched (in the words of writer Carolyn Geer) "ten living, breathing *Fortune* readers, all of whom fantasize about retiring not just comfortably, but while they're still young" with leading financial experts who "devised detailed, personalized plans for each individual or couple, with the goal of having them quit the rat race early—or at least years ahead of what they might have expected."

Even then, I remember, the financial advisors we called were a gloomy lot. Had our early retiree hopefuls thought about health-care costs, given that they wouldn't qualify for Medicare for decades? Did they realize that stocks might not always go up 25 percent a year? Nonetheless, some of the advisors gamely offered suggestions for our early retiree hopefuls who also wanted to send kids to Harvard, start businesses, or in the case of Dida Kutz, a 40-something tech writer I interviewed extensively, scuba dive in Malaysia, courtesy of the stock options being doled out like candy in Silicon Valley at the time. I've since learned from conversations with financial planners that these gloomy assessments are part of the job. No matter how much you've stashed away, your financial advisor is going to tell you it's not enough, and given how *little* most people have stashed away, she's probably going to be right. Financial planners describe people who walk in at age 45, have $80,000 in savings, and want to retire at age 55 with six figures of retirement income per year. So, they ask, what stocks should I be buying? As if what's standing between them and their goal is a mere matter of asset allocation.

Anyway, we offered our advice. Our early retirement package ran on August 14, 2000. Then, over the next year and a bit, the stock market proceeded to go on a deep-sea dive of its own. *Fortune* tracked down some of the early retirement hopefuls two years later to learn that they'd scaled back these plans. Dida Kutz, for instance, saw her tech firm go belly-up, as well as the next software company where she worked. She decided to start an opal distribution business, but initial costs for that had depleted her savings. As Janice Revell wrote in the 2002 follow-up article, "There is a problem with even the best retirement advice, a flaw that financial planners (and yes, magazine writers) routinely seem to forget. Even the most determined savers, even those with the smartest asset allocations, discover that something inevitably threatens their nest egg. Call it 'real life,' for lack of a better term."

I tracked down Kutz in 2011 and found that "real life" had continued with a vengeance. Following a series of devastating events (including a diving accident that almost killed her and a boyfriend's death in a sailing accident), she wound up taking a stable 9-to-5 job as an editor for the Defense Language Institute in Monterey, California. It wasn't scuba diving in Malaysia, which our original article claimed she would be doing by 2005, though, following her marine tragedies, she had avoided water sports for a long time. When we talked again, 11 years after our initial conversations, things were looking up. She was running a Web site devoted to diving, was volunteering at the Monterey Bay Aquarium, and was doing more research diving. She was also training to go into a different line of work that would allow her more flexibility for these different projects. "Retirement," however, wasn't a part of those plans. "I realize that I'm going to be working into my seventies," Kutz told me.

Yet despite these changed expectations, the idea of saving up for a secure retirement ("secure" meaning you'd have enough assets to quit working for good while withdrawing a principal-preserving 4 percent per year) has survived. *Fortune*, after all, still publishes an annual Retirement Guide—a perennial bestseller. In tough times, the articles simply change to talk about salvaging your nest egg or using a retirement calculator to get savings back on track.

To me, what's interesting about all this is how we got the notion of "retiring" in the first place. In the past, many people's retirement wealth came in the form of children who would take care of them when they grew old. This didn't always work, and poverty among the elderly has long been a social problem. As the modern state began to emerge, it became a policy problem, and in 1889, German chancellor Otto von Bismarck introduced the first old-age social insurance program. Contributions would come from employees, employers, and the state, and starting at age 70, workers would be eligible for a pension. Germany later lowered the age to 65, the same age President Franklin Roosevelt selected when he introduced Social Security in 1935. It would be a program of forced savings to guard against the hazards and vicissitudes of old age. These programs complemented the pensions that large employers started bestowing on retired workers around the turn of the 20th century.

In addition to guarding against old-age poverty, some policy makers saw another benefit to pensions. By giving older folks an income outside of working, you could bribe them out of the workforce, thus freeing up jobs for younger people. This "lump of labor" theory—the idea that there are a certain, nonelastic number of jobs in the economy—has been a persistent part of the cultural conversation, even though economists view it as a fallacy. One of the reasons Social Security benefits rose in the early years of the program, and the program soon allowed early retirement (at age 62), is that it was viewed as a win-win situation. Seniors could stop working, and their retirement (in theory) created opportunities for new hires.

Over time, however, all these programs have suffered from both demographic and financial issues. The U.S. birthrate fell from a high of close to four children per woman in the mid-1950s to well below two children per woman in the 1970s. Money that is paid into Social Security by workers is immediately paid out to recipients, rather than kept in individual accounts, and so to keep the program solvent, the population must have a high number of workers per retiree. But given the baby bust of the 1970s, the workforce is about to face a dearth of people who can support the baby boomers in retirement. Adding to this complication is the happy news that we're living longer. When Roosevelt created Social Security in the 1930s, life expectancy at birth was 58 for men and 62 for women, though the Social Security Administration is a bit touchy about this point, since it implies that FDR built a system that most people would pay into without getting a penny back. As the SSA notes, these low numbers reflected widespread infant mortality that, in an era before adequate antibiotics and vaccines, even an organization like Van Ginkel's Every Child Succeeds couldn't have done much about. Still, these days, there is a higher proportion of those who make it to age 21 then make it to age 65. People who make it to age 65 in good health can reasonably expect to live to age 85 or more.

Twenty to thirty years, or even forty years on occasion, is a long time. Promising such defined benefit pensions to employees has strained the finances of many a company now competing in a less closed and cozy world. Some discharged them in bankruptcy. Others struggle to provide them. Many stopped, and most new companies never started, partly because of the expense and also because the labor market has changed. Pensions work best in an environment where people stay with companies for decades. These days, few people do that, and the corporate life cycle may also be shrinking. As one young Google employee told me, he cannot imagine that Google will be around in its current form in 50 years. After all, 50 years ago, there wasn't much of an Internet to be searched, let alone personal computers that allowed people access to it. We have no idea how we'll get information 50 years from now and whether a company like Google will be part of that, or even exist. So how would a pension work in that situation? This young employee preferred the defined contribution model, e.g. 401(k)s. Such plans help employees save for retirement, often with matching funds from an employer. Unlike with a pension, however, the employee owns the capital no matter the length of his tenure and can easily take the money with him when he changes jobs. These days, the majority of the U.S. labor force has a 401(k) or similar plan.

In theory, the 401(k) should allow anyone to build up a nice nest egg. It is a staple of personal finance literature to explain how, by documenting the miracle of compound interest over a 40-year horizon (or longer). In Dave Ramsey's *The Total Money Makeover*, for instance, he gives us "Joe and Suzy Average" who invest $7,500 per year ($625 per month) using their tax-free retirement account. They do this from age 30 to 70, getting 12 percent interest per year. At the end, they have $7,588,545 to their names. Ramsey notes that this might be optimistic: "What if I'm half wrong? What if you end up with only $4 million?" The point, of course, is that this is still a lot more than most people manage to amass. Ramsey says he uses the 12 percent figure because "the stock market has averaged just below a 12 percent return on investment throughout its history." During a recent 40-year period, 1970–2009, the S&P 500 returned 10.38 percent annually, even including the massive 2008–2009 crash, so that sounds reasonable. In *The Automatic Millionaire*, personal finance guru David Bach suggests that people can save even smaller amounts and still build up millions if they start early. If you assume returns of 10 percent per year, a 15-year-old could save $3,000 a year for five years, then not touch the money or add anything to the pot, and return at age 65 to find $1.6 million sitting there.

These are large sums, and these charts on compound interest are always motivational, but there are a few things to keep in mind. One is the effect of inflation, which can take a bigger bite than you might think. Investing $3,000 a year now, as Bach suggests, seems quite doable. This is less than $10 a day. Cut out a few coffees (the lattes he made famous), lunches, and mall trips and you could find the cash. Saving $7,500 per year would be more aggressive, but this is still just 15 percent of a midlevel household income of $50,000. If you were getting a 50 percent employer match in your retirement fund, then you'd have to save only $5,000 per year to get those same returns. Again, this seems doable.

To think about the issue of inflation though, consider this: saving $3,000 a year back in 1970, for a nest egg to look like the numbers Ramsey and Bach cite now, would have been a very different matter. The average household income then (in 1970 dollars) was around $9,000 per year. Telling a young person then to invest $3,000 per year would be much like telling a 22-year-old now "Hey, all you have to do to have a secure retirement is invest $17,000 to $18,000 per year!" This is true, but not necessarily that helpful. In terms of household income, $7,500 would have a sticker value of around $40,000 today. Very few people in their early 20s can sock that away, even with an employer match. They may be able to later in life, but the issue with compound interest (as Bach accurately points out) is that the bulk of the gains come from money put in at the beginning. Saving $40,000 in 2009 would do less for your upcoming retirement than saving the equivalent $7,500 in 1970.

To make the retirement math generate big returns despite inflation, you need a very high-paying job in your early 20s, and you have to save the bulk of your take-home pay during those youthful years when you are paying off student loans and/or raising children. Few people can do this. Some can, of course. Some high-income families manage to invest large amounts even as the breadwinners are quite young, but the long-term financial security of high-income families who save most of their money wasn't in doubt. The promise of personal finance literature is that *everyone* who saves and invests small amounts can have a high-seven-figure net worth over time. I am not so sure that's true.

Second, another caveat with these numbers is that, as any investment guide tells you, past performance is no prediction of future returns. The period 1970–2009 saw some dips (like 2008–2009), but it also saw an incredibly long and not particularly anticipated bull run. After the Black Friday crash in October 1987, people were loath to predict big returns. A 1988 *Money* magazine article on where to invest in the 1990s quotes one outlier economist trying to stir up the pot by claiming that the Dow could rise to 5,000 or 6,000 by the end of the decade.

It closed on December 31, 1999, at 11,497.

Sadly for those of us who started investing not long after that, it closed on December 31, 2010, at roughly the same place (11,578). So will we see the kind of growth we saw from 1970 to 2009 over the next 40 years? Maybe. Long term, the stock market has posted annual returns of about 6–7 percent when you adjust for inflation. That's much better than a bank CD, and any individual investor might do better than average. But if you want to be reasonably sure of having big amounts in the bank, you're going to have to save big amounts, because the difference between 6 percent returns and 12 percent returns is huge, and even over long periods of time, you might not hit that 6 percent. My husband and I have been diligent savers and investors over the past 10 years for me and 20 years for him. Two decades starts to resemble the "long-term" picture financial planners talk about. We've built up a solid financial cushion, which I'm grateful to have. Nonetheless, I can attest, looking at our brokerage statements, that the majority of what we've put away has come from our labor, and not from compound interest. Looking back at the previous chapter, I think the least painful way to save more is to earn more. Regardless, saving small amounts gives you, when you take into account inflation, modest amounts of wealth. Even over a long time horizon. Modest amounts of wealth cannot easily support 20 to 30 years of not working.

Moving over to the real world, the situation gets dicier, because we find that most people aren't even on track for modest retirement savings. Current 401(k) balances are nowhere near where they'd be if people had been saving even small chunks of their average salary at a young age—something the Employee Benefit Research Institute's annual Retirement Confidence Survey makes clear. In 2011, EBRI found, some 56 percent of workers had less than $25,000 in savings and investments. Some of these workers have an excuse: they're 22 years old. But the picture doesn't get rosier as people get older. Only 19 percent of people over age 55 had more than $250,000 in assets (not counting their primary residence). Adding to this problem, these days, savings accounts and CDs are yielding interest rates in the 1 percent range. Retirees who've put most of their nest egg in safe investments, and are pulling out 4 percent annually, are watching their capital disappear.

What all this suggests is that most people will find it difficult to save up enough of their income from ages 25–65 to live to age 85 or 95 with no new money coming in. Social Security will help some, but given the program's looming financial problems, it's not clear how helpful that income will be for many future retirees.

RETHINKING RETIREMENT

But enough of that gloom. This is a book about happiness. So here's a different question: why are we so into this idea of retirement in the first place?

The answer seems obvious. Who wouldn't prefer leisure to labor? Almost everyone talks of wanting to retire someday, and pretty much every major financial decision the experts tell us to make is designed with this goal in mind. We talk of building up wealth so that at some point we can stop working, preferably when we're young enough to enjoy ourselves. Ads for financial planning firms tend to feature mature but definitely not decrepit couples, purposefully staring at whatever ocean vista their wealth has afforded them.

Yet we seem conflicted about this. Surveys of Americans find that two thirds of adults say they would continue to work even if they won the lottery. This question has been asked in many surveys over the years, and stubborn majorities of us continue to proclaim we would not want to be idly rich.

I've been scratching my head for a while trying to figure out how these two beliefs fit together. Building up $5 million in retirement savings and winning $5 million in the lottery would enable the exact same life.

So why are we so fixated on saving for a leisurely retirement when we wouldn't use a windfall to live a life of leisure now? The best explanation I can see is that people believe if they won the lottery and became financially secure they'd be able to do work they loved in a flexible way. They wouldn't have to think about money first. They could seek out work that offered meaning and pleasure.

If that is the case, though, then the lure of retirement is not a statement on work in general. It is about quitting the work one is currently doing. So perhaps we are asking the wrong question. Rather than fixating on "retirement," why not put that same mental energy into figuring out what kind of work we'd never want to retire from?

This brings us back to Judith Van Ginkel. I was introduced to her after she won a $100,000 Purpose Prize in November 2010 from an organization called Civic Ventures. This nonprofit encourages seniors to pursue what it calls "encore careers." These are meaningful, flexible jobs that promote the greater good and, in many cases, the older person's finances as well. The idea is to tap the expertise of our most seasoned workers in ways that fit the more relaxed (or at least flexible) lifestyle many people desire in their golden years. Veteran businesspeople can advise new entrepreneurs. Educators can coach rookie teachers or design curricula. Health administrators can help people with chronic illnesses navigate the system. Obviously, many of these jobs can be done on a volunteer basis, which some seniors do, but even if you don't have to work, income is nice. It makes life more comfortable to pay bills without pulling money out of savings and worrying that interest rates are stuck at 1 percent. Indeed, contrary to the "lump of labor" theory, when seniors have more and more regular income, they'll spend more, which boosts aggregate demand and creates opportunities for other people. A 65-year-old living on a dwindling nest egg probably won't hire contractors to remodel her kitchen. A 65-year-old who's still working 30 hours a week just might.

The benefits don't stop there. When seniors continue to work for organizations—particularly in leadership roles (which are likely to be paid jobs)—they also create economic growth through the deployment of their incredible networks and skills. That's what Tim Will, the 63-year-old executive director of the Foothills Connect Business and Technology Center in Rutherfordton, North Carolina, has done. After he'd worked in the telecommunications industry for years, Will and his wife bought a 45-acre plot of land in this Appalachian community with the goal of starting an organic farm—a passion he'd picked up decades earlier in the Peace Corps. He hunted around for a teaching job to support this endeavor financially. As he met with principals, though, he soon realized that the community was still relying on dial-up Internet access. He took a job at Foothills Connect, where his first major project was "getting the leadership of the community to see that they would remain a third world county unless they got broadband," he says. With his telecom background, he was persuasive, and the community soon landed a grant for entering the 21st century.

With fast Internet access in place, the benefits started accruing. Like much of Appalachia, Rutherfordton had lost jobs in the textile industry over the decades but was too far away from Charlotte or Asheville for easy access to those job centers. "Now, people can have businesses in their houses," Will says. He's overseen the incubation of several small companies, such as a CPA software firm, a Web design company, and a Web-based large-animal medications business. With access to online information, the local schools are starting to place better in Future Farmers of America soil judging competitions. And Will decided to use the community's swift online access to create a local organic farming industry. He taught local farmers organic methods (such as using chickens to kill pests and fertilize the soil) and then set up a virtual "Farmers Fresh Market" for them to sell their goods to Charlotte restaurants and high-end consumers who want to eat local and organic but (wisely) realize farming is not a personal core competency. His farmers' chicken sales alone now top $250,000 a year, to say nothing of the cheese, beef, produce, and so forth. His experience made this economic growth possible. "I would not have been able to do this when I was 30 because I would not have had the patience," he says. It is also unlikely that any given 30-year-old would have deep expertise in farming *and* telecommunications *and* management, *and* the ability to persuade a community that one's ideas are worth listening to.

I love this concept of encore careers. Of course, I *do* understand the appeal of taking a "gap year" or so around retirement age to do all the traveling, golfing, and just sitting on the porch and relaxing that one might not do with a full-time job. Sydney Lagier spent four years at an accounting firm and then 18 at a venture capital firm, before achieving her goal in 2008 of retiring in her 40s (age 44, to be precise). She tells me that "I highly recommend retiring full-time for at least a year, if not two, before incorporating work into the mix. That may not be possible for a lot of people sticking with the same type of job as they did during their careers, but I think it's worth just feeling what your life feels like without a job before jumping back in." Lagier has no trouble filling her days. She loves that her self-esteem is no longer wrapped up in what her bosses think of her. "When I retired, I realized my self-esteem was 100 percent influenced by me now and I loved that." Nonetheless, she still finds herself doing some freelance work. Forty, or maybe even 50 years "is an awful long time to go without ever working again." She doesn't need the income, but "I've also learned that the real draw of working for me was that I need to make myself do something outside of my comfort zone every so often," she says. "In retirement, you get to do all the things you want, and most of them aren't hard, they are enjoyable. But it's good to be reminded that you can conquer challenges." She reports that "it's made me feel good about myself to be challenged in this way."

Yes, even someone who saved enough in her 20s and 30s to retire and live off her assets (including health-care costs) sees upsides to work. She reports that many of her blog readers (her blog is called "Retirement: A Full-Time Job") also want to incorporate work into their "retired" years. A growing number of us are thinking this way, especially as we find that work need not mean drudgery. Rather than being something we dread or merely deign to do, it can be a major source of joy in our lives. As Suzanne Braun Levine, a cofounder of *Ms.* magazine, said once of baby boomers, "we have come to our 50s and 60s with a real appreciation of work. I don't think there's been a generation that has had so much experience with the concept of valuable work and the rewards of valuable work."

Those of us who can view our work this way are obviously privileged. I love writing, and it makes me incredibly happy to crank out articles and books, but I have done other jobs that I definitely have wanted to stop doing, like slapping garlic butter on breadsticks at Fazoli's Italian restaurant as a teenager. Then again, someone who owned an Italian family restaurant and worked with her children to lovingly re-create dishes from the old country might enjoy a good garlic slapping. We live in a delightfully varied economy, and if you have a solid education and a reasonable dose of ambition, there is likely some kind of work that would make you feel the way Judith Van Ginkel does about hers. "I never get up and feel, oh, I have to go to work today," she says. "I get up wanting to do this."

The happiest people I know have figured out what they love to do so much they'd do it for free—and then have figured out a way to get paid for their avocation. Finding such work is, of course, hard labor in and of itself. It means a long process of getting to know your quirks and your dreams and observing when you are happiest, or trying different things until you hit that sweet spot. It often means taking risks—sometimes to start a business or to take over a flailing organization that you know you could remake with a grander vision in mind. I don't know any way to make this all easier. But I do know that any hours invested in the pursuit are worthwhile, because when work is a source of joy for its own sake, you don't calculate how many pennies you'd need in order to spend your last few decades on the golf course. You may build up massive amounts of wealth. Why not? Wealth is a blessing and enables many things. But no matter the size of the pile, you'd want to keep working until health issues prevented it—admittedly, something that many of us will face as we get older. But saving for a few years of ill health that precludes almost all work at the very end of our lives is a different matter from saving for 20 to 30 years when we could work but don't. And "health issues" are sometimes more nuanced than they appear. If you love your work, you will find ways to do it even as physical limitations kick in. In *The Creative Habit*, choreographer Twyla Tharp writes of realizing that "nearing my sixth decade, I could no longer rationally harbor illusions that I was the only one who could perform my work. In fact, I couldn't. If I could, it would not have been challenging enough for my extraordinary (read: younger) dancers." But she could hire 20-something dancers to try out the moves she had in her head, and thus continue to work in a brutally physical field long into her 60s.

There is a fascinating gender dimension to these changing notions of retirement as well. The idea of working straight through from your 20s to your 60s, and then stopping, may be more the male norm than a female one. Partly this is because women live longer, and hence can still have a lengthy retirement even if they work into their 70s. But also, many women—like Van Ginkel—take time out earlier in their careers to raise children. Van Ginkel didn't get her PhD until her daughter was in school. When you start a career at age 37 and continue until age 72, you end up working just as long as someone who starts in his early 20s and retires at age 59. Even those of us who've worked for pay through our 20s and 30s have often forgone projects or overtime hours as we've cared for our babies. Life can throw curveballs, but I'm pretty sure I'll find it easier to work 50 hours a week at age 62 than I did at age 32. As women become a higher percentage of the workforce, this may change how we think about the cycles of work and life.

Of course, just because people want or need to continue working (or both) doesn't mean it will be easy. Over the past decade, many people in their 50s and early 60s have become retired involuntarily. According to a 2007 McKinsey Consumer Retirement Survey, some 40 percent of retirees said they'd been forced to leave the workforce earlier than planned, usually due to a health issue or layoff. Neither would necessarily preclude finding work again (if the health issue could be accommodated), but job-seeking seniors report rampant age discrimination among hiring managers. This overall climate discourages those laid off in their late 50s from trying to find something else.

There are ways to combat this, though, if people decided it was a serious policy goal to keep seniors in the workforce. Andrew Biggs, former principal deputy commissioner of the Social Security Administration (now at the American Enterprise Institute), has floated an intriguing idea of reducing the Social Security tax rate on workers who are over 62 years old. Not only would this make the system fairer to them (currently, older workers receive very little in additional benefits if they decide to keep paying into the system), it would give older workers a little more money in their pockets and would make them cheaper to employ. This could counter the age discrimination such workers now face.

Even without this, though, plenty of seniors maneuver around discrimination or inflexible workplaces by starting their own businesses or working as independent contractors. There are plenty of ways to work that don't involve reporting to a cubicle, factory, or store from 9 to 5, Monday through Friday. Self-employment, for instance, can give seniors the ability to scale up or down if they wish to travel, spend time with family, or train for triathlons.

Regardless, the encore career movement is growing, and garnering support from people of all political stripes. When I wrote about this for *USA Today* in early 2011, R. Albert Mohler Jr., president of the Southern Baptist Theological Seminary, seized on my line that "the notion that work is something you want to stop doing is getting a makeover."

"It's about time," he wrote. "The Bible dignifies both labor and age, but the modern American ideal of retirement is nowhere to be found in the Scriptures. Instead, lives of useful service to the Kingdom of Christ are the expectation, all the way to the grave . . . The idea for Christians should be redeployment, even after employment. There is so much Kingdom work to be done, and older believers are desperately needed in this great task."

And hey, if Kingdom work can pay the bills, too, it's win-win.

A BETTER REASON FOR WEALTH

All this said, whether you plan to work into your twilight years or not, it's still important to build up savings—though not necessarily to finance a traditional retirement. A more potent motivation is what even modest wealth (say, two to three years of your family's living expenses) buys you in the here and now.

Namely, it buys you freedom. Having money means you don't have to think about money, or at least you don't have to think about money first. This is the appeal of the retirement concept—that you don't *have* to do anything. But there's no reason to experience this freedom only at the point that you become intrigued by early bird specials. Assets can buy you the ability to walk away from a job or renegotiate its terms at age 35, not just age 65, if you decide you want to try something else—perhaps something you'll never wish to retire from.

I always love interviewing people who have built up such a "freedom fund" and then made life changes as a result. Antranig Garibian is a lawyer in Philadelphia. He'd been at his firm for seven years (five as an attorney) and things were going well. But then in mid-2010, he decided to divert cash into an emergency fund. "Whenever we received cash back on a credit card, tax refunds, gifts, discounts, bonuses, et cetera, we pretended like we never received it," he says. "That money adds up over time." The goal? Starting his own firm. He wasn't sure he wanted to continue specializing in defense for asbestos litigation suits (his firm's focus) long term, and he wanted to manage his own client relationships. He built up enough to cover all his bills for quite a while. Then he went in to give his notice. "They were somewhat shocked," he says. When he spoke with the senior partner, the man told Garibian that he had a future with the firm and discussed various opportunities, though Garibian wasn't quite sure what he wanted to do.

Then, around this time, he and his wife learned they were expecting their first child. This raised the stakes on walking away from a secure paycheck, although Garibian knew he could still do it. But then his firm approached him again about staying. "I conveyed my concerns with them about the nature of the practice and my desire to diversify," he says, and "we came to an understanding that the firm's resources would be available to me to market my own clients and to diversify my practice." Essentially, he could "build my own practice within the practice" and thus have the best of both worlds: "the security of the firm and the opportunity to be an entrepreneur and develop my own client base." Having a freedom fund gave him the ability to negotiate from a position of strength—a much better situation than many new fathers find themselves in as they contemplate how they'll support their families.

Others use their freedom fund to try a lower-paying career. Robert Pondiscio worked as the communications director for *BusinessWeek* during the heady days of the dot-com advertising boom. Rather than spend the bonus cash that all those JDS Uniphase ads brought in, he saved it, which supported him while he took an 80 percent pay cut to work as an elementary school teacher at P.S. 277 in the South Bronx.

It was a meaningful but tough job. In particular, he grew frustrated that he couldn't devote as much time to nurturing his high achievers as he wanted. And so, five years in, he realized he wanted a career that combined education, with a focus on high achievers, and communications. He began doing (among other things) PR for Prep for Prep, a program that prepares bright minority kids for admission to prep schools. Even though he has transitioned out of teaching for now, he's glad he did it—and knows that it wouldn't have been possible without a cushion. Indeed, his daughter's private-school tuition alone was more than his take-home pay from the teaching job.

So how do you build up a freedom fund, or a fund for anything that really matters to you? And how do you do it without forgoing all the little pleasures that can boost happiness? Articles on saving are inevitably dreary, because they focus on not doing things—not going out to eat, not shopping, not getting your nails done. It's hard to live in the negative. In the trade-off between present and future happiness, is a dinner out now more pleasurable than three dinners out at age 70? I'm not sure there's a right answer to that question. And so, I think the best way to save is not to focus on cutting small pleasures.

Instead, keep your structural expenses (housing, cars) low as a percentage of your regular income, so you don't have to worry about trivial expenses like lattes, even as you're still putting money away. If your base income is too low for that to work, then look at ways to make more money. Lots of extra money if you can. This bonus money will be relatively easy to save.

That's the approach that Crystal Paine took recently when her family was nearing a major savings goal. Paine's husband, Jesse, runs his own law firm, and Crystal is known online for her blog, "Money Saving Mom," which—impressive for a coupons-and-deals blog—acknowledges the opportunity cost of time. Paine sets a "minimum wage" of $20 per hour for her to deem any particular frugal practice worthwhile. That's why she doesn't bother making her own tortillas. But here's something she did want to do: pay cash for a house. That sounds crazy, but she had two advantages. First, her family lives in suburban Kansas, where you can get a decent house for about $150,000. Second, her family set their expenses very low, not becoming particularly dependent on Crystal's blog income, and didn't scale up expenses as her blog traffic began to soar. Eventually she was bringing in "more than a full-time income," she says. Since this was all extra cash, it was relatively easy to save, and Crystal was able to bank the full cost of a house in about 21 months—something she never could have done, she notes, if she'd just been trying to save a little bit more at the grocery store.

Owning their home outright—as young people—gives the Paines the kind of freedom that most people can't even imagine. Pretty close to anything coming in after taxes is theirs, to continue amassing wealth and to continue providing a cushion as they both run their own businesses. It doesn't feel nearly as risky to run a business if you don't have to pay a mortgage or rent! Their work allows them a lot of flexibility for spending time on other things. Like their three kids. Indeed, Crystal is homeschooling the brood.

In other words, the Paines have used their money to make sure they can continue doing the kinds of jobs that make a person feel lucky. Just like Van Ginkel. "People look at me and say you're nuts," Van Ginkel says of her long days and seemingly boundless energy for figuring out better ways to serve Cincinnati's young families. But "I love what I do. I work with bright people. We're doing good work." That sounds like a lot more fun than golf today, golf tomorrow, or golf at any time, frankly.

SPENDING

CHAPTER 4

Laughing at the Joneses

In the first years of the 20th century, cartoonist Arthur R. Momand surveyed his Long Island neighbors and made an observation. Many seemed to be living beyond their means in an effort to acquire what others had, jumping into a never-ending cycle of spending that gained steam as Americans started deeming single-family homes, cars, and other consumer goods as necessities. In his late 20s, Momand created a comic strip to lampoon this tendency. For several decades the strip ran in newspapers across the country, and American readers followed the domestic exploits of the McGinnis family and their unseen but oft-referenced neighbors. The title of the strip? *Keeping Up with the Joneses.*

The phrase lasted longer than the cartoon, drifting well into the modern world where we try to keep up with the Kardashians or, in extreme cases, the Gateses. It means different things to different people, but when you picture the Joneses, they aren't living in a modest bungalow and biking to work. No, they own a stately home with a manicured lawn surrounded by a wrought-iron fence. Their long driveway loops in front of the house so they can display some sleek black or silver luxury car—a good whose value stems partly from the fact that some versions signify more status than others. As we saw in the introduction with the designer label experiments, human beings are wired to seek and defer to status. This is particularly true when it comes to things other people can see. Who knows if your marriage is better than anyone else's? Who knows if your potluck dinner with friends was more enjoyable than someone else's picnic? These things are not easily compared, but one house is clearly bigger than another, one car more expensive, one flat-screen larger and more high-def. Our tendency is always to spend more on these visible markers than on nonpositional goods. Conspicuous consumption is human nature.

And so, in 2009, the average American family spent just over 50 percent of their total expenditures of $49,067 on housing and transportation (which comes out to 39 percent of the average pretax household income of $62,857). One can certainly imagine that lower-income families would need to spend a high percentage of their money simply to afford basic shelter and bus fare. But what's most fascinating is that (according to 2006 numbers from *Forbes*), while the poorest 20 percent of households spend 52.6 percent of their outgoing cash on housing and transportation, the richest 20 percent spend 47.8 percent. We are all hovering around the 50 percent mark.

Why is that? To be sure, people in the top 20 percent pay more in taxes and save more, so they spend a lower percentage of their income than people in the bottom 20 percent do (in the *Forbes* numbers, the richest 20 percent earned $132,158 and spent $83,710; the poorest earned $9,156 and spent $17,837, a feat made possible by transfer payments such as Social Security). Still, it's a bit of a head-scratcher why 50 percent is the right amount of one's outgoing cash to put toward housing and transportation, no matter what one earns. We are talking roughly $9,000 vs. $40,000 for the bottom and top income quintiles, which are very different numbers to have arrived at this magical percentage. It's also curious when you think of all the things money can buy beyond houses and cars that people in the top income brackets could devote more money to if they wished. Education. Art. Charity. Travel. Spa visits.

Yet somehow 50 percent sounds about right to people. But here's a question to ask yourself: if you are in the top half of the income distribution, where more flexibility is possible, how would your life change if you decided to spend 40 percent of your budget on housing and cars, and devoted that additional 10 percent to something else? Let's say you're already saving religiously. What if you spent 30 percent of your budget on these necessities and 20 percent on other things? What kinds of choices would that enable?

There are many reasons families spend what they do, but I still think, as we look at the intersection of money and happiness, it's worth reexamining our relationships with our houses and our cars. The simplest reason is that these are our biggest expenses. Many frugality tomes and television segments center on food, entertainment, and clothing, because these are perceived as costs that can quickly be changed. This is true, but the problem, as we saw in earlier chapters, is that these items make up small percentages of people's budgets and are often not worth the forgone happiness to change. Spending less on housing and transportation, on the other hand, can make big life changes possible.

I was reminded of this recently when I interviewed Kristen Hagopian, a Pennsylvania mom of two who's written a book called *Brilliant Frugal Living*. Her family successfully transitioned from bringing in $100,000 a year to $50,000 when she quit her job to stay home with her kids. So she's been the subject of much media attention, usually centering on her trips to discount grocery stores where she finds Starbucks coffee for $4, bags of tortilla chips for 35 cents each, boxes of Cheerios for $1.75, and Ghirardelli chocolate for a song ("I will not

buy cheap chocolate. Life is too short and I will not do it," she says).
She shops at well-stocked Goodwills and purchases secondhand
Louis Vuitton purses—often with the tags still on them—for mere
dollars. But a family can't go from $100,000 to $50,000 just by cutting expenses that amount to a mere 5 percent (for clothes) and 10–
15 percent (for food) of most people's budgets. So I asked Hagopian
about her house and cars. She paused because, as she told me, no one
ever asks her about that. It turns out that her family owns their me-
ticulously maintained 2000 Lincoln Town Car and 1992 Dodge
Spirit outright and—wisely—bought a house they could afford on a
$50,000 income, not the $100,000 they were making. In other words,
groceries and secondhand Louis Vuitton bags had little to do with it.
The Hagopians could hack their income in half because they had no
car payments and a 50 percent cheaper house than a real estate agent
would claim they could afford.

Obviously, housing and transportation expenses are hard to
change in the short run, and selling a house incurs massive transaction costs. But if you're serious about using cash for things that bring
you the most pleasure, or if you do want or need to cut back a lot, why
not look at what these large outlays are doing for you? Maybe they
are achieving worthwhile goals. Many people consider houses to be
assets, which is why spending a high percentage of one's income on
a home seems justifiable. But maybe they are not. The last few years
have certainly shown the downside of thinking that more house is always better, even if you have to stretch to afford it. Regardless, it's
silly to talk about personal finance without talking about where you
live and what you drive. In the context of achieving happiness, there
is also some intriguing research suggesting that big, infrequent purchases (such as houses and cars) don't do much for overall happiness,
whereas spending a lower percentage of your income on these items
might free up cash for categories that *will* give you a more pleasant
life. There are also plenty of people who have discovered this truth

and, rather than trying to keep up with the Joneses or submitting to their tyranny, are getting a good laugh on them.

THE AMERICAN DREAM

When I started writing this book, the issues surrounding what we spend on houses, cars, and yards were largely academic to me. Then, in the course of cranking out the manuscript, I went from being a New York City apartment dweller and subway rider to the owner of a suburban house with a yard, the possessor of a mortgage, and the driver of a car. And so, while faxing signed forms back to the mortgage company and later running around my new and more rustic neighborhood in Pennsylvania, I spent a lot of time pondering why we make the financial choices we do.

Our decision to become suburban homeowners had been percolating for a while. Like many urban couples in the breeding stage of our lives, my husband and I had grown weary of some of New York City's challenges. In our last Manhattan apartment, our two boys shared a bedroom, which is common in expensive urban areas but strikes many non–New Yorkers we know as strange, given what we were paying in rent. My office was a chunk of our bedroom. Eventually, our 1,500 square feet began to feel tight. And so, as often happens, potential ownership of a detached single-family home beckoned.

But why, exactly, was it beckoning? This question, at least until recently, hasn't been asked too much. Home ownership is widely touted as the American Dream, an "axiomatic good," as *Time* magazine put it in the fall of 2010.

It remains wildly popular, deemed worthy of scrimping. According to that same 2006 *Forbes* article on how Americans make and spend their money, the 30–35 percent of our budgets we now spend on housing compares with just shy of 15 percent in 1960. The most popular reasons for home ownership, according to Fannie Mae surveys, are access to good schools and safety for one's family.

There is some research, often touted by real estate agents, supporting the idea that home ownership is a good thing. This ranges from higher voting rates among homeowners to higher high school graduation rates among their children, though some of this seems to be more correlation than causation. Home owners may be more involved in their communities, not because they're better people than renters but because they move less frequently. One reason they move less frequently? The high transaction costs of paying a Realtor when you sell a house.

Still, there are likely some real benefits. When you own something, you take better care of it. A home can be used as collateral for a loan and as a way to build wealth. Perhaps because of these benefits, the U.S. government grants home ownership lavish subsidies. Not only is most mortgage interest deductible, government guarantees in the secondary market for buying and reselling mortgages (in the form of Fannie Mae and Freddie Mac) have historically kept interest rates lower than banks would set on their own. Home ownership is, culturally, a sign of responsibility, even though it's also, usually, a sign of debt. Tell people you're saving up for a down payment on a house and they'll nod; say you're saving up to put $40,000 down on a $200,000 stock portfolio, and they'd think you were nuts. Actually, they'd probably call the Securities and Exchange Commission (SEC), since securities rules require you to put more money down when you're initially buying on margin. Think about that. During the height of the housing boom, people were putting far less than 10 percent down on houses, but other investments have stricter rules, even though a stock portfolio can be liquidated in bits and pieces—thus letting you hedge your bets—and a home cannot. If you hit tough times, you can't just sell your bathroom.

Whether or not we think all this through, big chunks of us—

some two thirds of Americans—buy. I am now, for the first time, part of that percentage. My husband has had the more unusual experience of going in and out of it. He bought a 900-square-foot one-bedroom condo in New York shortly before we got engaged. It was perfect for two newlyweds but a bit tight for the three people we soon became. We put it on the market when we decided to have a second kid, and sold it at the absolute bottom of the real estate bust, in winter 2008–2009. Since we couldn't decide if we were staying in the city or going, we rented a two-bedroom apartment elsewhere in the same building. Eventually, in the spring of 2011, we started looking in the Philadelphia suburbs, since my husband's work had migrated there, we were expecting a third child, and the process of finding a kindergarten in Manhattan appeared more complicated than my memories of applying to college. In early March, we met with a real estate agent on the Main Line and tromped from house to house, where I promptly became enamored of just how much square footage I could get for the after-tax equivalent of my New York City rent. I began to see why people buy baby monitors: in 1,500 square feet, when the baby cries, you hear him. During one open house, I lost my three-year-old in many thousands of square feet of residential expanse. But I have to say, after years of living on top of one another, of having other family members deposit their toys and dirty underwear next to my desk, I was ready to spread out a little. More than a little.

Multiply my sentiments by millions of other young families, and you can see why ever-bigger houses have conquered the real estate market as SUVs have conquered the road. "I think it comes from the history of this country—moving out west into this great uncharted territory," says Sarah Susanka, a Raleigh, North Carolina–based architect. "Somehow in this country we have the notion that more space is freedom. It's associated in our minds with expansiveness and opportunity."

More opportunity certainly sounds better than less opportunity, and so, while new single-family homes in the early 1970s averaged around 1,600 square feet (with a median of around 1,500), this ballooned to 2,521 (median 2,277) by the top of the housing boom in 2007. On the high end of the market, 10,000-square-foot homes are not unusual, even if some of the names assigned to what are really just random rooms (video library? computer loft?) require much creativity from people who write real estate listings. The median price rose from $23,400 in 1970 to $104,500 in 1987 (the first year it crossed six figures) to $247,900 in 2007 (before falling to $221,800 in 2010), faster than inflation and faster than wages—a bit of alchemy made possible by bargain-basement interest rates. When interest rates are low, the incentives to raise your monthly payment a wee bit are strong. Financial writer Liz Pulliam Weston ran a chart in one of her columns showing that if you were willing to spend 25 percent of a $45,000 income on housing, you could borrow only $128,745 (figuring in property taxes and insurance). If you were willing to spend 33 percent of your income, though, you could get a loan for $181,582. This is quite a bit more house for an extra $300 per month, with the existence of 30-year mortgages pushing buyers toward spending those extra dollars on the margin. All the way up the line. Assuming you've got the cash to put 20 percent down, with low interest rates, the difference between a $1.25 million house (with a $1 million mortgage) and a $2 million house ($1.6 million mortgage) can be an extra $4,000 per month, which wouldn't seem huge if you have $400,000 sitting around for a down payment. Since interest on the first $1.1 million borrowed is deductible, the numbers look even better.

A big house, of course, means a big lawn. As we pondered our move to the 'burbs, we started judging homes based on the amount of sod in the backyard, because another axiom of American living is that a growing family needs some grass. But lawns, too, are a relatively new phenomenon—something growing families did without for much of human history. Historians aren't sure why lawns became as closely tied to the American Dream as home ownership itself. Perhaps early suburban sorts wished to mimic the look of British castle grounds, minus the sheep responsible for the close cropping. The fad spread, and now millions of acres of the United States are covered with grasses that wouldn't grow well here if left to their own devices.

As people require bigger homes, they've generally moved, by extension, farther away from places they need to go. Our suburban move was the exception, since it brought my husband closer to his office and clients. But this is not usually the way it works. The average commute is now hovering at about 50 minutes per day (25 each way). People with train commutes tend to like them. People with car commutes, not so much. Driving itself is not unpleasant, but driving when other people are driving means battling traffic. We naturally adapt to most things that produce a steady state of unpleasantness or pleasantness. The push and pull of traffic, on the other hand, means every day is a new hell. Perhaps to ease the pain, we seek out more comfort in our cars—more space for hauling supplies in the back, more cup-holders, and movie screens for the kiddies, something I found myself considering in the vehicles I was looking at, though as a child I managed to survive long car trips without them.

The ironic thing about the big suburban house, the lawn, and the cars they require is that the daily activities these widely desired goods thrust upon us are pretty low on the human enjoyment scale. According to a 1–10 scale of human happiness produced from the 1985 Americans' Use of Time Project, while gardening is quite pleasant, yard work scored a 5.0—not far above going to the dentist (4.7). Cleaning the house scored a 4.9, and commuting landed at 6.3. These are all below playing sports, experiencing art or music, watching TV, exercising, and playing with kids. In the 2004 study of Texas working women that I've referred to in previous chapters, commuting and housework ranked near the bottom of the happiness scale for these women's days.

So if housework, yard work, and commuting make us miserable, or are at least far enough down the happiness scale that we could envision better ways to spend our time, why do we pursue big, expensive houses with grassy yards that require rush-hour driving? Some explanations center on policy choices, such as a bias against mixed-use development, heavy federal subsidies for road building, and educational choices that have made urban schools unattractive to middle-class parents. When I've raised this question with people, the school issue is the one they most frequently cite. Good school districts will likely be more expensive than bad school districts, and housing sizes and prices will be bid up as higher-income families (who have seen big gains in income over the last few decades) become willing to pay more. Some economists such as Robert Frank, author of *Falling Behind: How Rising Inequality Harms the Middle Class*, pin a big portion of escalating home debt on the desire of middle-income families not to consign their children to inferior schools. Which makes a lot of sense. Access to good schools was a major reason we bought where we did. On the other hand, the same school district can have wildly varying prices (not to mention rental units if you don't want to buy). In Lower Merion, Pennsylvania, for instance, when we were looking in spring 2011, you could buy a three-bedroom home within walking distance of public transportation into Philadelphia for $165,000. You could also buy a home for $3 million or more. Good schools are not the whole explanation. I put a lot of stock in the "axiomatic good" theory. Everyone wants it, so therefore it must make us happy.

It's important to keep in mind, though, that happiness is always a battle against adaptation—that is, getting used to things, so they no longer bring us the happiness they once did. In a 2010 paper surveying dozens of experiments, professors Elizabeth Dunn, Daniel Gilbert, and Timothy Wilson identified several recurring themes of how money can encourage happiness—and how it can not. One key theme? "As long as money is limited by its failure to grow on trees, we may be better off devoting our finite financial resources to purchasing frequent doses of lovely things rather than infrequent doses of lovelier things," they write. "Indeed, across many different domains, happiness is more strongly associated with the frequency than the intensity of people's positive affective experiences." Good sex three times a week is better than mind-blowing sex three times a year. Variability also forestalls adaptation, and small, repeated pleasurable experiences are more likely to be variable than big infrequently purchased objects. "Having a beer after work with friends, for example, is never exactly the same as it was before; this week the bar had a new India Pale Ale from Oregon on tap, and Sam brought along his new friend Kate who told a funny story about dachshunds. If we buy an expensive dining room table, on the other hand, it's pretty much the same table today as it was last week." A car at least has the virtue of being able to bring you to new and exciting places—one reason that one study of older Americans found that vehicle spending was associated with happiness—but any functioning car can do that. A house doesn't change much and soon becomes the expected norm.

None of this means that spending money on houses and cars is wrong. We all want pleasant transportation and pleasant living quarters. I know I do. The problem is when we overspend on the house and the cars, beyond what would satisfy us for comfort, functionality, and safety, to the point where we don't have money for other pleasures. The difference between spending 33 percent of one's income on housing and 25 percent is 8 percent to spend on other things. That's $4,000 on $50,000 and $8,000 on $100,000, which, in the context of buying happiness, can cover a reasonable number of dinners out, movie tickets, weekend trips, or even a cleaning service to free up time to enjoy all these experiences. Or consider this: if you need to save more, and earning more isn't an option, cutting out those dinners, movies, and weekend trips requires daily doses of self-discipline. This is a virtue that, alas, most of us have in short supply.

Whereas buying a cheaper house (or car) requires only one episode of self-discipline. After that, you're good for years.

And then there is the matter of freedom. Spending half your budget on housing and transportation locks you into that level of income. What if you want to take a career risk, go back to school, or just take a sabbatical? A rainy day fund can cover a while, but bigger house and car payments deplete such a fund faster than smaller ones.

As part of our cultural reckoning, though, we are reexamining all our financial commitments and goals. There's been a small backlash against home ownership itself. Leverage can juice returns, but what people forgot prior to 2007 or so is that this works in reverse, too. If your $200,000 home declines 10 percent in value before you've paid much on the principal, and you've put 10 percent down, you've lost 100 percent of your equity. As people have started to do a more serious risk analysis on home ownership than the mortgage mills used to do, Fannie Mae found a slight decrease, in recent years, in the percentage of renters who think owning is better than renting.

NOT SO BIG

I suspect home ownership is so ingrained in the American psyche that its prevalence won't decline much anytime soon. Many of us do like the idea of having a place that is ours—a place we can have bookshelves built in if we want, and where the landlord can't renovate in a way that gives us less closet space. Also, if you rent, there will never be a point where you can stop paying rent, but if you buy, you could certainly pay off a 15-year mortgage in 15 years, or earlier. Or you could pay cash in the first place. Owing nothing beyond property taxes, insurance, and utilities creates incredible freedom— and is the quickest way for most people to get housing expenses down to as low a percentage of income as possible.

But there has definitely been a backlash against larger homes that require a stretch to afford. A summer 2010 survey from real estate listing service Trulia found that, among Americans who viewed home ownership as part of the American Dream, only 9 percent said their ideal house would be larger than 3,200 square feet. An equal 9 percent called 800–1,400 square feet perfect. By 2009, the average new home size had drifted down to 2,438 feet, and then down to 2,392 in 2010.

As usually happens when a huge trend reverses, even slightly, feature writers make a big deal about it. And so newspaper readers have been treated to several articles lately about very tiny homes.

Jay Shafer, owner of the California-based Tumbleweed Tiny House Company, features prominently in many of these stories. Shafer announces proudly on his Web site that "since 1997 I have been living in houses smaller than some people's closets." The homes he designs range from 65 to about 800 square feet—and with lots of design detailing, often look like cozy little dwarf cottages.

When I called Shafer, I learned that he's lived simply for decades. Years ago, he spent summers teaching at a camp on Long Island, where he lived in his truck and "didn't miss anything except for a toilet" (a laptop would have been nice, too, he notes, but they didn't exist then). Until recently, he had been living in a sub-100-square-foot house, but when he and his wife had a baby, they moved into a 500-square-foot model, which is like a "mansion for me." His old house sits next door—a detached version of a man cave.

His customers are a diverse lot. Some are downsizing seniors, while others are "creative types, people who are doing things, and want to do those things rather than paying a mortgage," he says. "Mostly what you get with a small house is freedom." That doesn't mean they're cheap. An 8-by-12 house can run $40,000, "which is a lot per square foot" because they "still have all the expensive parts," like a kitchen and bathroom. So even if you park your tiny house on a vacant lot in the middle of nowhere, you'll still be paying roughly half the going rate per square foot for luxury condos in Manhattan. On the other hand, $40,000 is pretty affordable when it comes to a place to live. The energy bills can be as little as $8 a month, plus "you get rid of all that stuff you don't need," says Shafer. A 100-square-foot house cannot hold most of the trappings of modern life. So you don't acquire them. You spend your money on experiences instead.

This minimalist philosophy is a big part of the appeal, says Kent Griswold, proprietor of the Tiny House blog, who spends his days posting photos of houses like Shafer's. On a recent day, highlights included a log cabin with a stone chimney and a very tiny porch in the coastal mountains of northern California, a small teak house barge for sale in the Seattle area, and an essay about the huts of the Buryat farmers in Tunkinsky National Park in Siberia. Griswold has found enough of an audience among the tiny house obsessed, he tells me, to make "some decent money" from his work. For most people, houses that small are pure fantasy, and Griswold himself lives in a 1,200-square-foot castle. "The extreme tiny houses are more of a movement," he says. "But downsizing is more of a trend." Even if the vast majority of us have no interest in living in a 100-square-foot house, we are entertaining the idea that bigger by itself isn't always better. Better can be better—and sometimes can even be cheaper.

At least that's the message that has pushed Sarah Susanka's design books (*The Not So Big House*) up the bestseller lists. She notes that in many larger homes, the formal dining room, living room, and cathedral-like front entryway are used a few times a year at most. These rooms can easily add up to 1,000 square feet or more of unused space. Ditto guest bedroom suites, exercise rooms, and other square-footage inflators. Early in her career, Susanka would meet families who wanted her to design additions, yet they would have three or more rooms that were completely unused and sometimes devoid of furniture as well. She would point out the disparity, and her clients would shrug. Those rooms were unusable and were there only for resale value. "How much money gets wasted in almost every house—every new house particularly—for a room that is built based on fantasy or the needs of a bygone era?" she muses. Empty living rooms still have to be heated, cooled, and cleaned. A guest bathroom built at the cost of $15,000 might be used three weekends a year. "Per flush, that ends up being pretty expensive," she says.

After a few years of hearing home owners' odd requests, Susanka began to "ask people to consider how they actually live as opposed to the way they think they are supposed to or imagine they'd like to live in an ideal world." The goal is to "use every square foot every day," and use the money you save to add great design details and character.

This often means dispensing with a formal dining room. Skip the formal living room, Susanka suggests, and just have a comfortable family room, ideally within sight of the kitchen. If certain family members have a tendency to watch TV or play video games in the family room, you can also have a nearby "away room" with glass doors where family members preferring quiet can sit and read—but still be near the action. Or alternatively, the kids and their noise can be contained in the away room, allowing adults to have a normal conversation without having to shout to make themselves heard. One of the reasons houses have gotten bigger is because people want to get away from each other's noise, but a pair of French doors that allows household members to feel connected while doing their own thing is a much cheaper solution. Although some people like the idea of acres of private space, "the vast majority of time in our homes is spent together," says Susanka. Indeed, she suggests, if houses shunt people off in different directions too often, they get lonely. With children, the need for privacy can be satisfied with bunk beds that have curtains, or little hideaways for each kid—reading nooks, or even a Harry Potter–style room under a staircase. If you can produce evidence that you have visited a gym at least twice a week for the past year, you can justify an exercise room. But "you have to be realistic about your life," Susanka says. "Just because you build a room doesn't mean you'll change your habits."

Susanka reminds homeowners that the money they save by buying or building a not-so-big house can go toward design details that not only make the house feel bigger than it is, but make them happier in it. Placing windows next to an adjacent perpendicular wall makes light bounce around the space, making any room seem bigger and brighter. Rather than putting a light fixture in the middle of a hallway ceiling, move it to the end to illuminate a framed poster or piece of art. Humans are drawn toward light, and "we end up liking the whole wing of the house accessed by the hallway" much more than we would with a central light, Susanka notes. The brightness at the end of the vista lifts our spirits. Varying ceiling heights and nooks can make a house feel simultaneously intimate and expansive. If you have fewer bathrooms, each one can have nicer fixtures; money not spent on a room you don't use can go toward silk pillows, rugs, and art that make your home feel like a luxurious retreat.

Of course, such trade-offs imply that you need to make trade-offs. Presumably, some of the folks who hire a star architect penning bestselling books do not. But Susanka reports that even her clients with unlimited budgets have told her that they "like their houses better when there is an everyday use for every space."

I certainly had these words ringing in my ears as we closed on a house that is, to be honest, not so small. It was within our comfort zone financially (one of the upsides of buying in a down market). But we wrestled with the question of square footage for quite a while. In my mind, at least, one reason for negotiating down the price and our interest rate was having money left over to pay for help with cleaning and maintenance. We looked at some equally priced houses that were smaller, but we didn't want to have to move again if our family kept expanding, and we like having grandparents visit us—something they are less inclined to do when forced to sleep on the sofa or a leaky air mattress. I'd spent days paging through Susanka's books before house hunting. And so I fell in love with our new home's architectural details: window seats, varying ceiling heights, fireplaces. These made the space feel cozy. Plus, while I like family togetherness as much as anyone, I'm a mom who works from home. Having separate quarters to conduct my business, including space for meetings and a backdrop for video interviews that does not involve a bed covered in dirty laundry, has a real upside for me. Indeed, we are turning the rooms that normally go unused in houses into the headquarters of Vanderkam, Inc. I know I'll be using most of those feet every day—so I hope Susanka would approve.

SEAS OF GREEN

Though the Joneses always have a spotless lawn and a riding lawn mower that costs more than a small car, a surprising number of people are rethinking their yards, too. I see the appeal of a spot for kids to run and play, or space for a garden or swing set, and our new home does have some grass, though I know that community playgrounds serve the run-and-play function nicely, too. In rethinking communities, one potential setup—the best of both urban and suburban worlds—might be a smattering of tightly designed houses ringing an enclosed central square. Porches could face this green where kids would always have others to play with, better playground equipment than most families would buy on their own, and neighbors willing to split the labor or cost necessary to maintain such a space.

In the absence of such redesigned communities, some people decide to forgo grass completely. Consider the story of Diane Faulkner, whose lawn was always causing her trouble. This Jacksonville, Florida, resident traveled frequently, and in her absence, her thirsty, fussy grass would go brown or otherwise run afoul of her neighborhood association's rules. She hated returning home to a $50 fine, but the last straw was when her travels took her to rural Kenya. Immersed in local life, she'd wake up at dawn with the villagers to walk miles along a dried-up river toward a water source, then return with a few gallons for cooking and washing. "That was their whole morning," she says. As soon as she got on the plane back to the United States, she had a thought: "How many gallons of water do I waste on that stinking lawn?" More broadly, why did she have a lawn to start with? A field of green, closely cropped grass is the default landscape for a "nice" neighborhood, but it's not as if this is some divinely ordained zoning code.

From an environmental perspective, there are also plenty of reasons it shouldn't be. Homeowners have a tendency to use massive amounts of herbicide, often to kill "weeds" such as dandelions and clover that look just as green as grass when you mow them. Mowing itself—in the modern, mechanized format—requires fuel, just like driving, with the added downside that people refuel mowers in their driveways, not professionally operated service stations. So fuel gets spilled and runs into the water supply. And all these woes are before you even get to the issue of water. By some estimates, maintaining nonnative plants requires 10,000 gallons of water per year per lawn, over and above rainwater.

For all these reasons, municipalities such as Raleigh and Los Angeles regulate how many times a week homeowners can turn on sprinklers. Big chunks of Canada have banned certain lawn pesticides. But rather than spend tax dollars enforcing regulations, another approach would be for people to think of lawns as a fashion—a fashion much like wearing the feathers of rare birds in hats was once a fashion. Fashions can change when enough people decide they are ridiculous. Few parents would light a cigarette at a playground anymore, even if it's not illegal. Likewise, the presence of a vast, green, weedless lawn in the middle of summer may one day be viewed the same way: as a weird and antisocial thing.

There are certainly options that won't make a house look like an abandoned property. Anyone with a lawn can decide to have less grass by keeping a patch around the house and turning the rest into a meadow that attracts birds and butterflies. Our new house has a lot of ground cover that grows well in eastern Pennsylvania—vines, trees, and other plants—in part to minimize the area that needs active maintenance. Looking at this varied greenery out my office window is far more pleasant than looking at a monotonous sea of green. Planting a garden is a reasonable option, as long as you enjoy time spent gardening (which many people do) and take care not to plant even thirstier species. The least subversive option is to swear off herbicides and let the grass go dormant during the summer.

Others go all out, gleefully joining the "kill your lawn" movement. California resident Anne Severs planted her 2,500-square-foot all-native garden in 2003, and her home is now a regular stop on the Bringing Back the Natives Garden Tour in her area. Her colorful yard features monkeyflower, coyote mint, manzanita, California fuchsia, woolly blue curls, and buckwheat. Severs doesn't have to water in summer, and some clever use of mulch keeps weeds from soaking up her time. "If I'm out there, it's to gaze upon the beauty," she says.

Faulkner likewise ripped up all her sod. She redid her lawn with rocks and hearty plants such as Confederate jasmine, arranged to look like an English garden. Because all her plants grow well in Florida, they require no upkeep. None. "I don't have to mow, I don't have to water, I don't have to trim," she reports. Her water bill has gone from $80–$90 per month to $20, to say nothing of the fines she no longer has to pay.

THE ONE-CAR QUESTION

The car is the last element of the Joneses trifecta—those possessions that inspire us to compare ourselves with others. Are cars necessary? I know most people outside New York and a few other dense urban areas can't ditch them completely, though the growth of Zipcar, Hertz on Demand, and other car-share services is making a "car-lite" lifestyle more possible. Now that these companies exist, people can take public transportation or bike to work, and then borrow a car for weekend grocery runs, dentist trips, or out-of-town excursions. Zipcar spokeswoman Colleen McCormick tells me that the company's members report saving, on average, about $600 per month compared with owning a car. While the average household spends 15–20 percent of its budget on transportation, Zipcar households spend only about 6 percent. What else could $600 a month buy? That's two plane tickets from New York to California, a weekend of spa treatments, or the monthly salaries of five librarians in a remote Moroccan village. And that's while still having a car when you need one!

Even if we're not prepared to share with strangers, many of us could save on the cost of car ownership by driving our vehicles for longer. Carl Texter, the chief financial officer of Cardinal Logistics Management, drives an Acura that is 10 years old. He's thought of buying a new car and could certainly afford one, but isn't sure he could find a reasonable one that's "as nice as the one I have now." Well maintained, "those cars will last a long time," he reports. Having no car payments frees up money for him and his wife to do other things, such as take vacations at the very swanky Anse Chastanet resort in St. Lucia, where they went recently. Many of us could also spend less on gas and maintenance by taking fewer trips in our cars. Tom Vanderbilt's fascinating 2008 book, *Traffic*, made the case that road demand is highly elastic. We don't necessarily drive because we have places to go. We go places because we have cars and nice, user-friendly roads that lead us to their parking lots.

So here's a brainteaser for the average two-car family: how would you function if you could have only one car? The first few days would be chaotic and involve a lot more schedule coordination than most families are accustomed to. But soon you'd start carpooling to work, either with each other, or colleagues, or neighbors who work nearby. Mornings might start featuring a family trip to drop the primary breadwinner off at a train station, and evenings a trip to pick him or her up. Your kids might take the bus, carpool, walk, or bike to school. Potentially they'd be in fewer activities, but playing chauffeur to children all afternoon and weekends is a major source of parental unhappiness. You might not spend as much time shopping for stuff, but most of us don't need more stuff. As one of my blog readers told me, "we like having just one vehicle because it encourages us to be more strategic about planning outings—whether to the grocery store or to see friends—which saves time and money." Long term, one or both of you might negotiate the ability to work from home more often, or you'd move someplace closer to work and schools, which, by cutting commuting time, would make the average person much happier. Moving closer might mean more expensive housing, but as we saw earlier, for $300 less a month in car payments, insurance, and gas, you could borrow more than $50,000 extra on a mortgage while holding total housing and transportation costs constant.

Of course, there would be downsides, too. Another blog reader noted that her family had one car for years because she could walk to work and drop her daughter at day care on the way there. Her husband worked farther away and drove. Trouble arose, though, whenever her daughter got sick and had to be taken to the doctor. The parent who was closest didn't have a car at her disposal to drive there.

This would be a hassle, and is one reason that our suburban

move involved buying two cars, though I can work at home and our home is within walking distance of a grocery store, post office, elementary school, and so forth. I assumed that my husband would take the car in a one-car situation, and I didn't like the idea of having to ask him whenever I wanted to go somewhere (though during the transition when we did have one car, he made sure to leave it with me, and called taxis to take him anywhere that I couldn't easily drop him off). Emergencies are also a convenient reason for two cars, though emergencies are also a good time to lean on neighbors and extended family.

Nonetheless, as I can see in my own thought process, we have a tendency to value freedom and flexibility and build our lives around these possibilities, even when we rarely require them. I laugh now that I once viewed 24/7 access to the storage facility we rented for some belongings years ago as a major selling point. The only times we showed up were when we moved the stuff in and moved it out. Likewise, you can see this in the nascent marketing for electric vehicles and the issue of "range anxiety." This is the worry that you'll run out of juice before you get to a plug. The range of the Nissan Leaf is about 100 miles, farther than 90 percent of us drive on any given day. But in the back of our minds we have this notion that maybe today, despite our usual habit of driving to work and home, we'll hit the open road and cruise to Atlantic City. You can't do that in an electric car, or if the carpool is waiting for you, or if your family will be meeting the 5:45 P.M. train at the station. It's a fantasy, just as the formal china many engaged couples register for is a fantasy of what married life will require. Fantasies are fine, but problems arise when we mortgage our present happiness in anticipation of them. Spending $100 less per month on cars—possible by driving less or driving the cars you have longer—frees up funds for a latte a day. Telecommuting once a week would free up 50 minutes to enjoy a latte, as would living in a slightly smaller house five minutes closer to work.

Or you could figure out how to chuck the house and car payments entirely—as Sherrie Tingley has done.

Tingley and her husband are both in their 50s. They used to live in a suburban home outside Ottawa, but the 40-minute car commute to downtown was a big drain on their happiness. "It didn't feel like we had a life," she says. Hanging around downtown after work meant a late night, and there wasn't much to do where they lived. So in 2000, they purchased a duplex in a transitional neighborhood close to downtown for $116,000 with an $87,000 mortgage. With a combined six-figure income, they could have afforded a lot more than that, but they wanted to be able to manage on either of their salaries, in case one person lost a job or if either party wanted to quit. They lived in the top half (about 750 square feet) and rented out the bottom. As their incomes went up, they devoted the extra money to the mortgage and paid it off in five years. Then they started saving up for a renovation and converted the two units into one single 1,400-square-foot house, which Tingley claims now feels almost too big. They ripped up their grass. "We see no use for a lawn," she says. "They're stupid, unless you're lawn bowling." The trees and patio that took the lawn's place provide a nice relaxing spot for hanging out during the time they're not stuck in traffic.

Indeed, around this time, they started walking to work together, turning their commute into a daily date. They enjoyed it so much that "we started questioning if we really needed the expense of having a car and decided that at the next major repair we would get rid of it," she reports. They bought bikes and a carrier for hauling things, and sold the car in August 2008.

Now on weekends they bike to the grocery store together. "Once in a while we run an errand by bus and it feels like an adventure," she says. "Financially, we are saving a bundle of money." Last year they spent a total of $600 on car rentals for trips out of town. Plus, "I realized that a lot of the shopping we did before was a waste of time," and "we would buy things that we did not really need." Now Tingley does most of her shopping online, far more deliberately. With few housing and car expenses, life maintenance runs them $2,000 a month—much of which is spent on fun line items like eating out, travel, and entertainment. Tingley is on track to save $70,000 per year. She's putting that in her "freedom fund" to buy the ability to do whatever she wants soon.

All in all, it's a pretty plush life, lived entirely within her means. An acquaintance who was considering getting Tingley's particular Visa card recently asked about the interest rate. Tingley confessed that she had absolutely no idea, because she'd never had to pay it. "I don't want to be the Joneses," she says. There's no point trying to keep up when you're thrilled with what you've got.

CHAPTER 5

The Best Weekend Ever

We watch a lot of *Dora the Explorer* in my house. I usually try to escape and read the newspaper while my children stare at the TV, but one fall day not long ago I became quite intrigued by an episode called "Boots's Special Day." In this episode, Boots, Dora's monkey sidekick, could celebrate his "special day" by doing whatever he wanted. Like any child not accustomed to dimming his exuberance, Boots had no problem figuring out what that would entail. He and Dora marched in a drum parade, visited Dora's cousin Diego's Animal Rescue Center, where they got to meet a banana bird (a nice reference to the monkey's favorite food), and then visited Boots's daddy at the amusement park where he worked. Along the way, they got ice cream, and rode on a tugboat and fire truck. At the end of each episode, Dora and Boots talk about their favorite part of the day. In this episode, Boots announced that today was all his favorite things.

This story got me thinking. What would it be like to fill a day, or even better, a whole weekend, with one's favorite things? How would one do that? What are those favorite things? And most important for the sake of this book, what would that cost?

The answer turns out to be $200. Or at least that's what it was for Jennie Aguirre, a Goodyear, Arizona, resident who volunteered for my experiment to help figure out the answer to this question. Her assignment: plan a weekend she would remember for a long time and figure out how much it cost. She was a good guinea pig. For $200 she danced, she ate, she shopped, and she got together with friends. Indeed, Aguirre thought that with a bit of creativity, she could have done things even cheaper. But what she and I learned about buying happiness is that strategy matters as much as the amount spent. Whether you have all the money in the world, or something more limited, her techniques are replicable for anyone looking to have "an absolute blast," as Aguirre gushed in a post-weekend e-mail.

EXPERIENCES VS. THINGS

Over the past few years as I've been writing and speaking about how people spend their time, I've done a lot of "time makeovers" in which I have volunteers keep a log of exactly how they spend their hours every day for a week. Then I help them figure out ways they can use their time more effectively. I usually start by asking people what they want more of in their lives. This is a trickier question than it sounds. Many of us ponder what we'd like to spend less time doing (usually driving and emptying the dishwasher), but not what we'd prefer to do with the time we'd save. To help people think through that question, I've borrowed an exercise from career coach Caroline Ceniza-Levine called the List of 100 Dreams. This is a completely unedited list of anything you might want to do or have in life. People start off with grand dreams, like visiting the pyramids in Egypt, but as we get closer to 100, of necessity we start brainstorming more everyday fonts of joy, like visiting an art museum an hour away, or having dinner with a close friend once a week.

After reading through several of these lists, I've noticed a theme: many items mentioned lean toward the experiential side. This was true for Boots's special day as well—it was full of fun experiences, rather than acquiring stuff like new toys. The monkey was on to something. "When something is sitting on your shelf, you get used to it very fast," says Sonja Lyubomirsky, author of *The How of Happiness*. "It doesn't give you the same thrill anymore," whereas a memory can be savored and enjoyed over and over.

Of course, it's not that stuff necessarily makes us *unhappy*, though some people aren't willing to take that risk. Poke around online and you'll soon discover a small but serious subculture devoted to minimalism—having as few things in one's life as possible. Nina Yau, 26, previously of Chicago, writes the blog Castles in the Air. She decided in the summer of 2008 that "I didn't want to be bogged down by my stuff anymore." Mired in a stressful job, she felt she had very little control of her life. But she could control what was in her apartment. She looked around and saw "all this furniture I had in my apartment that I don't need. All these clothes I never wear that I don't need. I just don't need it, so what's the point of having it?" She started unloading it all. First, on Amazon and Craigslist she sold movies, books, and the Backstreet Boys CDs she'd collected as a teenager. She made a lot of money, and "that felt really good." So then it was off to her closet, where she started giving things away to friends and a local shelter. "I just pared down," she says, and eventually she committed to owning fewer than 100 things. She began posting lists of all her possessions on her blog, continually reevaluating what she had. "Sometimes you get busy and things can start to accumulate without you even realizing." So she would pare down again, lower and lower, until finally, when she moved to Taipei for a while in early 2011, she took just 34 things:

1. MacBook Pro, 13.3"

2. Camera, Sony Cyber-shot DSC-T99

3. Journal, Moleskine

4. USB Flash Drive

5. Passports

6. Headphones

7. Linen bag, Green

8. Messenger bag, Green

9. Wristlet

10. Eyeglasses

11. Sunglasses

12. Bikini, Purple

13. Jacket, Black

14. Jacket, Green

15. Hoodie, Gray

16. Bras (grouped as one item)

17. Socks (grouped as one item)

18. Underwear (grouped as one item)

19. Jeans

20. Sports capris, Black

21. Shorts, Black

22. Dress, Gray

23. Skirt, Gray

24. Tank top, Black

25. Tank top, Green

26. Tank top, Gray

27. T-shirt, Natural

28. T-shirt, Black

29. T-shirt, Gray

30. Heels, Black

31. Vibram FiveFingers, Black

32. Sandals, Brown

33. Flats, Black

34. Boots, Brown

All this fit in two small bags, and she relished being able to do whatever she wanted to do without having to worry about her stuff. "It gives me so much more freedom," she says. By consciously choosing to have fewer things in her life, she was able to make both Taiwan and the United States her home bases, moving effortlessly between them in a way that those of us whose moves require boxes, trucks, and teams of men can barely fathom. By not buying or maintaining stuff, she was able to spend more on travel and flitted to eight countries between January and June 2011. These experiences "give me so much more abundance and happiness in life than any material good" might, she says.

Yau's beliefs are deeply held, so I will be curious how long she can continue living this way. I know from personal experience that it becomes much harder to maintain minimalism when other people come into your life. I try to purge my possessions as often as possible, but our hand-me-down tub of Lego Duplo blocks alone contains well over 100 items.

I also think that the dividing line between stuff and experiences is more nuanced than absolutists make it out to be. Is buying a tent spending on stuff or experiences? It's an object, but it enables a camping trip. A book is an object but hopefully an experience, too, as you curl up, read it, and transport yourself to a different world. One of my favorite possessions—something I'd include on a "best purchases ever" list—is a set of patio furniture that has enabled my family to eat, read, and socialize outside since we moved to Pennsylvania. You probably have items that you'd include on a "best purchases ever" list, too. On the other hand, unpacking dozens of boxes in my new home soon reminded me how much glassware, shirts bought on sale, and conference tote bags I'd accumulated over the years—items that bring me no pleasure whatsoever and feel leaden sitting in closets. So in general, the point still holds. You may be better off spending less on the tent (as long as it's good enough to work) and putting the savings toward taking an extra camping trip. There are also other ways to spend less money on (or devote less space to) stuff while still enjoying what stuff enables. A Kindle can hold a shelf's worth of books. Smart neighbors could start a lending library of sorts for things no one needs frequently. A whole block of people who know and trust one another can own a nice lawn mower, snowblower, camping equipment, infant toys, DVDs, tools, and party supplies (like a 30-cup coffeemaker) in common. With the money you all save, you can actually throw the kinds of parties where you might use a 30-cup coffeemaker. That would be a good trade-off. We anticipate experiences, enjoy them while they're happening, and then enjoy the memories later. This is true of once-in-a-lifetime experiences (like visiting those pyramids) but also for more mundane fun events—like that trip to the museum or hike in the park.

So when I talked to Aguirre, who works for the online Western Governors University, is married, and has a 13-year-old daughter, I asked her the first question for creating a great weekend—a question that acknowledges the primacy of experiences in human happiness:

1. **What activities do you enjoy most?** These can be whatever you want, of course, informed by your List of 100 Dreams, but happiness research gives a few guidelines. The study I keep referencing of Texas working women, published in *Science* in 2004, found that, beyond obviously pleasurable activities like eating and sex, most of us are happiest when we are socializing, exercising, or engaging in spiritual activities. If you think about it, this makes sense. As Lyubomirsky notes, these activities tap into our basic needs. "One need is connectedness, to spend time with others. Then competence—we want to be competent and want to master things, then autonomy—feeling like you're the captain of your own ship." Exercise challenges our bodies in pursuit of competence and autonomy, and releases natural endorphins. To really bump up the happiness factor, exercise outdoors. A variety of studies find that we enjoy exercise more in the fresh air and are more likely to repeat it. Volunteering, worship, or other spiritual activities challenge our souls, while being with other people makes us feel part of something larger than ourselves.

Aguirre spent some time brainstorming and then told me that "I have always wanted to try a cooking class. I love to dance and have taken dance classes before . . . I love to shop and I really enjoy game nights with friends. I have recently discovered a love for karaoke and at our last few gatherings we rented a machine . . . one of my favorite activities is bike riding, my husband enjoys it but our 13-year-old usually complains. I would love to go on a long bike ride somewhere, we talk about it but never do it."

None of these activities seemed like they'd break the bank with the possible exception of shopping, depending on how it's done. Aguirre promised me she'd be smart. But if you're concerned, it may help to list ways you could do your favorite activities on the cheap. For instance:

▸ If you love movies but don't care about seeing a specific one, you could go to a free screening at a nearby university, or catch a flick at a second-run theater.

▸ If you want to get together with friends for a meal, you could host a potluck rather than go to a restaurant.

▸ If you love to shop, you could set up a clothing swap with your friends and "shop" in each other's closets.

▸ If you love to travel, swap houses with someone or choose a destination close by.

▸ If your favorite part of a vacation is the hotel, stay in a fabulous one in your town, spend the whole day in the spa, and order room service—but skip the airfare.

After Aguirre came up with her desired activities for a great weekend, we proceeded to the most important step for building more happiness into one's life, asking the second question:

2. **When, exactly, can you plan time to do these things?** I'm a planner, so planning fun events well ahead of time makes intuitive sense to me, but I didn't know why until I did some more research into the field of positive psychology. As I was writing an article for *Prevention* on this topic of creating a great weekend, I learned that having specific things to look forward to massively increases your enjoyment of them. "It extends the experience," says Cassie Mogilner,

a professor of marketing at the University of Pennsylvania's Wharton School, who specializes in happiness research. "The whole time you're looking forward to it and anticipating it, you're getting some of the benefits of the experience itself." This is one of the reasons why people love vacation travel. You generally have to figure it out at least a few days ahead of time. Indeed, research published in the journal *Applied Research in Quality of Life* in 2010 found that vacation anticipation boosted happiness levels for eight weeks—an argument for planning more shorter trips rather than a few longer ones. Plan a four-day weekend every other month and the happiness boost could last all year. I know this anticipation factor is why I always have great birthday weeks. Not only do I think ahead of time about what I'd like to do—meeting up with friends, taking the kids somewhere fun, getting a massage—I plan these activities in advance and then enjoy seeing them on my calendar, knowing that tickets are purchased and babysitters are booked.

We looked at Aguirre's calendar and aimed for the weekend of January 28–30, 2011. Before we could plan specifics and logistics, Aguirre went off and signed up for a cooking class that would start in the spring, so she decided to hold off on cooking plans until then. We talked about doing a karaoke night on Friday, but it turned out that most bars in the area viewed karaoke as a midweek way to fill their establishments (I had to give her points for trying: she had friends calling all around Arizona). Beyond her normal weekend activities such as sleeping and going to church, here's what her plan ultimately looked like:

- ▸ **Friday:** happy hour with her husband, then a night out dancing with girlfriends.

- ▸ **Saturday:** bike ride

- ▸ **Saturday night:** game night with friends

▸ **Sunday:** a leisurely afternoon shopping

▸ **Sunday night:** crab legs for dinner (one of her family's favorite meals)

Aguirre was smart to limit her ambitions to a few activities. Even Boots's Special Day featured three main activities with a few pleasant diversions, rather than a death march through 10 events that leave you too exhausted to enjoy the last few.

She was also smart to plan something fun for Sunday night. "That extends the weekend," says Mogilner, the Wharton prof. Many of us, even if we like our jobs, experience the occasional bout of Sunday night blues. When you've got something on your calendar for that spot, rather than thinking about going back to work on Monday, you'll spend your Sunday afternoon looking forward to the evening.

Unless you want to hit Monday feeling like a train wreck, though, you should probably keep your Sunday night plans low-key. In the late summer of 2010, Holland Saltsman and John Buck, a St. Louis–area couple with two children, asked all their friends to pick fall weekends that worked for their schedules. For three months, they had a different family over for a casual dinner every Sunday night. Because it was a school/work night, everyone had a 7:30 curfew, but planning ahead gave them something to look forward to, and "we managed to cram a lot of fun and catching up into those few hours," Saltsman reports.

Of course, to truly enjoy your weekend, you also need to ask Question 3:

3. **How can you off-load the not-fun stuff?** Yes, your best weekend ever will still feature some "have-to-dos" on your list, even if it's just filling the car with gas or stopping by an ATM. Designate a two-to-three-hour block of time for your errands and other things that

have to happen. "This allows you to be in the present moment for all the other pleasant stuff," Mogilner told me. It's hard to relax if, in the back of your mind, you're thinking about all the niggling little things on your to-do list. Carving out chore hours lets you tell yourself that "there's a time for errands—and it's not that time." As a bonus, carving out a small window encourages you to spend less time on any activity you don't want to do. Ignore, minimize, or outsource instead. Outsourcing can cost money, but if you truly hate something, that may be a wise use of resources, perhaps the resources you save by buying less stuff.

And finally, as you're going through your great weekend, figure out:

4. **What is this costing and how do you feel?** Many times we spend money trying to make ourselves happy. But we're prone to, as one woman put it in a budget she sent me, "mindless shopping for crap." You go to the mall because you're bored. You spend $50 on things that just sit in the bag, when you could have spent $50 treating your sister to lunch at her favorite restaurant and enjoying an afternoon together at the art museum. Better to figure out for sure what will make you happy and how much that costs. Once you know this, you'll know exactly what it will cost to boost your spirits in the future.

That was certainly Jennie Aguirre's goal going into that late January weekend, which started off fun and went from there. When her husband came home from work on Friday ready for their planned happy hour, she intended to suggest their favorite sushi restaurant for a snack and drinks ("our 13-year-old loves California rolls but won't eat a hot dog"). Before she could mention it, though, he told her that her weekend was off to a great start because some friends gave him a late Christmas present: a gift card to that exact restaurant! Taking this as an auspicious sign, they enjoyed their (discounted) sushi, and while they were eating, Aguirre decided that "a trip to Baskin-

Robbins would certainly make the weekend better," so they went there for ice cream. Afterward, they took their daughter to a friend's house, her husband rented an action movie, and Aguirre met her girlfriends. "Dancing was a total blast!" she told me. The club had no cover and sold drink specials until 10, and since she was driving, that ensured that the booze part of the adventure was relatively cheap. Her Friday tally clocked in at $25 at the sushi restaurant, $9 on ice cream, and $4 at the dance club (a $2 beer and a $2 tip).

On Saturday, she slept in ("so wonderful"). The weather was beautiful, and she and her husband biked to their favorite bagel place, thus getting some exercise outside. "[We] really just took our time and talked the whole way." They spent $10 at Einstein Bros. Bagels, each ordering their favorite breakfast wraps and coffee. After biking home, Aguirre's husband took their daughter and a cousin to the mall while Aguirre compressed her errands and chores into a few hours—straightening the house ahead of company coming over, and picking up snacks and drinks for game night (the guests planned to bring things, too, so she spent $30 on beer, ingredients for dip, brownies, and chocolate-covered strawberries). Soon, friends and family started arriving, and they played Loaded Questions, a board game in which players have to guess other players' answers to such questions as "If you could 'dis-invent' one thing, what would it be?" and "What celebrity has no right being a celebrity?" Everyone stayed until midnight, laughing and chatting, with the kids playing their own games upstairs.

Sunday did not start as intended. "We had planned to go to church and rarely miss"—regular worship service attendance being a major source of happiness—"but we were both so tired from the night before that we decided to sleep in," Aguirre told me. This is one of the dangers of planning too much for a weekend. Any future game nights may have to end at 11 instead. But Aguirre soon got back on track, going to Dillard's Clearance Center for her shopping day. She needed to go to Salt Lake City the next week for meetings, and so wanted to get a few things, but the shopping trip was really more about the experience than anything else. She spent five solo hours shopping, and "I probably tried on 50 dresses" because "I was by myself and knew I could stay as long as I wanted to." She spent about $60 there and $25 at another store.

On the way home from shopping Aguirre picked up three pounds of crab legs for $8.99/pound, plus a lemon and a loaf of French bread. Her husband had already picked up peach pie and ice cream for dessert, so the bill for this special dinner came out to a bit under $40. They cooked their crab legs and savored this fun end to a full weekend.

"It was more fun than I expected it to be, and I realized as it was happening that the activities I chose were not things that would have been unusual to just happen spontaneously," she wrote in an e-mail afterward. "What I learned about the process is that it is much more fun when you plan the time and are really purposeful about how you spend it. It was exciting to be out on Friday night and look forward to the next morning and then go on a bike ride and look forward to our friends and family coming over and then have game night and think, hey, I get to go shop all day tomorrow!"

Originally, she had been calling our little experiment a "dream weekend," but then she and her husband decided that a dream weekend would be extravagant. It would include once-in-a-lifetime experiences, like jetting to Paris and having a private dinner in the Louvre or something else that you couldn't exactly repeat one month later. As researchers keep finding, happiness is more about frequency than intensity. This exercise "helps you think about the simple activities that just bring you joy," she said, "and they don't have to cost a lot. Heck, you could do this for free if you were creative!" Taking inspiration from the 1993 movie *Groundhog Day*, in which meteorologist Phil asks how he should live if he has to live the same day over and over again, Aguirre decided that if she had to live a weekend over and over again, this January weekend right before Groundhog Day would have been it. She decided to make "Groundhog Weekend" an annual tradition. It's her grown-up version of Boots's Special Day. Now she's really boosting her happiness by anticipating what she'll plan next year.

CHAPTER 6

The Marginal Cost of Children

Happiness is a complicated subject, especially when it comes to children. Do children make us happy? Our reflexive answer is yes. Some people have religious reasons for believing this—Psalm 127 tells us that "children are a blessing from the Lord"—and others simply note that modern inhabitants of rich countries don't have to have children, and yet most of them do. More than 80 percent of Americans will have at least one child. Most of us know how to avoid parenthood if we wish, and our economy is no longer based on the kind of labor-intensive farming that renders children a necessity. So it stands to reason that people have kids because they think life will be better with them than without them. Otherwise, we're all gluttons for punishment.

That seems like straightforward logic, but a few wags have delighted lately in claiming that, actually, we *are* pretty masochistic on this front. If you look at happiness as measured on a moment-by-moment basis, parents are not happier than nonparents. They are often mildly less happy. Indeed, child care ranks among the least pleasant activities of our days. It does not score far above commuting, which is saying something, though it isn't surprising when you think about it. Changing diapers is unpleasant. So is nagging a sullen teenager to do her homework. These parental duties are certainly less enjoyable than other things we could be doing with our time, like watching television.

On the other hand, watching TV isn't a fulfilling way to spend one's life, even if it's more fun than diapers at any given moment. Another way to think about happiness is in terms of overall life satisfaction—that is, whether you think you're living a good life or not. It seems reasonable that having children would correlate with life satisfaction, but those who have studied the relative happiness of parents as they increase their family size have shown that any reported positive effects are not statistically significant.

So if parenthood doesn't correlate with moment-by-moment happiness, or even overall life satisfaction, does that mean we'd be better off skipping it? Well, not so fast. One way to find out if forgoing parenthood is a wise choice is to ask people who don't have children what they think of that decision. A 2003 Gallup poll that surveyed childless adults over age 41 found that if they had to do it all over again, only 24 percent would have had no children. Nearly half (46 percent) would have had two children, and 15 percent would have had three or more. Parenthood may not make people happy, but, looking in the rearview mirror, few people think *not* having children was the right choice.

See what I mean by complicated?

Beyond the questions of measured happiness or regret, though, what I find most interesting, digging into these numbers, is that Americans show a slight tendency to have fewer children than we think is ideal. Gallup found that adults, overall, think 2.5 children is the right amount to have in a family, yet the American birth rate hovers around 2.1 children per woman. Some 37 percent of all adults think that the ideal family would have three or more children, yet according to 2008 census numbers, among women aged 40–44 (most of whom will no longer be adding to their families), 17.8 percent have had no children, 18.4 percent have had one, 36.2 percent have had two, 17.8 percent have had three, 6.1 percent have had four, and only 3.7 percent have had five or more. Those last three categories add up to 27.6 percent, which is a reasonable amount below the 37 percent who think three or more kids is ideal. Adults who have kids under age 18 at home are slightly more likely to believe having three or more kids is ideal (44 percent) than other people.

So, given that most of us take the plunge into parenthood, with its associated day-to-day lows, why do a significant number of people stop before reaching their ideal family size? Why do people who like big families have two children instead of three or more?

The reasons people have the number of children they do are as complicated as the happiness question. Some parents call it quits at two for environmental, practical, or health reasons. As the age of first marriage climbs, some parents start their families late enough that they have time for only two before their fertility window closes. Two is also a very strong social norm—that magical number at which clerks in the supermarket won't ask when you're having another, and people in the supermarket don't roll their eyes when they see you, obviously pregnant, chasing a preschooler and a toddler down the aisles.

But I think that financial considerations play a big role in this undershooting, too. In the United States, the birth rate fell quite a bit from 2007 to 2009 as the economy tumbled into recession. Kids, we know, cost money. A lot of money. They are tied with houses as the biggest-ticket item people spend their money on. In 2010, the median house price in the United States was $221,800, and the U.S. Department of Agriculture produced a report claiming that it cost $222,360 to raise a child to age 18. As the news reports based on that latter statistic always belabor, this doesn't include college. Somehow the average family manages to pony up for two of these luxury goods, but even if children are a blessing, we wonder who—besides movie stars and business moguls spreading their offspring over four wives—can afford to spend more than half a million dollars on kids?

Economics 101, however, suggests there's more to the math than simple multiplication. In most industrial situations, producing three of something does not cost three times as much as producing one. There are always start-up costs; make one car and you need to set up a whole assembly line. Make the second, and third, and fourth, however, and your infrastructure is already in place. As the start-up costs are spread out over increasing units, the marginal cost of each individual unit declines.

Kids aren't cars, of course, but they do require a known set of inputs. Shelter. Clothing. Food. Transportation. Education. Entertainment. Parental time. All these have costs. But are they the same for each kid, no matter how many kids you have?

The USDA numbers suggest not. In 2009, the USDA reported, a two-parent family earning between $56,870 and $98,470, with one 14-year-old, would spend $16,360 a year on that child's upkeep (including the extra space needed in a home to accommodate him). The same family with a 16-year-old and a 14-year-old would spend $26,620, meaning the second kid cost only $10,260. The marginal costs are starting to fall, though they are still high. But then, as the family continues to grow, the real magic happens. A similar family with three children—an 11-year-old, a 13-year-old, and a 16-year-old— would spend $30,450. In other words, the third kid cost a mere $3,830. Indeed, both the second and third kid together cost less than the first.

The USDA doesn't pursue this line of reasoning too far, but from conversations with larger families, I suspect the decline continues. I asked Chris and Wendy Jeub of Colorado, who have 16 kids, whether 16 was eight times as expensive as 2. "We would be flat broke if that were true," Chris told me. We ran through a few numbers, and it turned out that their monthly food bill was about the same as mine. Granted, I was living in Manhattan at the time of our interview, but even deducting a 50 percent premium for the land of $6 Crispix (and my nights ordering sushi), this implies that an expanding family can involve a pretty steep per person decline.

The question is, why do costs decline? The answer turns out to be twofold: larger families do indeed achieve economies of scale. But those with less than all the money in the world to their names also wind up making a lot of trade-offs, bucking various cultural expectations about what is good for children to have. This leads us to a second question: in the context of how we choose to use our money, particularly as we try to optimize well-being for ourselves and those we love, does it matter how much money we spend on each kid?

The answer, as with much about parenting, is complicated—though as with houses and cars, there's a solid argument to be made that spending big will not necessarily produce more happiness than spending as if you were having your third or fourth kid first, and that if you do think having three or more kids is ideal, money doesn't have to be the reason to stop.

CONTEMPLATING NUMBER THREE

In early 2011, Lisa Belkin, then with the *New York Times*, agreed to ask her Motherlode blog readers about the marginal costs of kids for me. As she put it in her blog, the question of whether economies of scale apply to families was "professional, yes, but also personal." My oldest son, Jasper, was in preschool. My second, Sam, was weaned and walking. I was pondering having a third, so Lisa wrote that I wanted to know, "is the third child somehow more 'economical' than the first or second?"

About a month passed between my initial e-mails with Lisa and the blog post running. During that time, I learned that, whatever the marginal costs turned out to be, my third child was already on her way. That knowledge made reading the comment thread an even more personal experience, as I found myself thinking highly *unprofessional* things about the commenters who wanted to change the subject from the microeconomics of the family to how my third child— hypothetical to them but real to me—was going to make life worse for everyone else. As one reader put it, "Each additional child takes away from another child already living in the world." One gentleman from Connecticut wrote, "in addition to the costs to the individual family, perhaps we should include the cost to the community and to the planet." He asked, "what does it cost the earth when we bring more than two children per family into the world?" What would the child's education cost our community? Since every kid is a tax deduction in the U.S. code, "how much do taxes for people with smaller families rise in order to make up the difference?" Within the first 24 hours of Lisa's post, 99 readers had recommended his comment, so I imagine many people agree that children (beyond that magical number of two) create externalities—negative externalities.

I am not so sure this is the case, and not just for my children, whose sheer cuteness is a positive externality if I ever saw one. The environmental argument has been around for centuries, and yet the world has not succumbed to the famine and pestilence people have predicted would come to pass by now. If anything, conditions are improving as human beings come up with innovative ways to grow more food and deploy modern technology. But even if my third child was a planetary catastrophe, I don't see how having two would be the moral solution in a world that already contains 7 billion other souls. Far better to have one or none. As for being a cost to the community, educated parents tend to produce offspring who go on to participate enthusiastically in the workforce, paying more in taxes than they consume in services. Three workers will pay more taxes than two workers. Four workers will pay more than three. Of course, that doesn't mean there aren't practical reasons to have fewer kids. They are a lot of work, particularly at the beginning, and require a lot of parental energy. But again, if one worries about this, then there's no reason to have two. Some recent studies have debunked most popular prejudices about only children being spoiled or maladjusted. Children don't need siblings to turn out fine.

But even if only children do turn out fine, many parents, it seems, would still like to give their children siblings. If the average woman has two kids, and our ideal family size is 2.5, that implies that a significant number of people have stopped at two, though they would prefer three (or more). As one Connecticut mom told me, "I know lots of people who regret not having a third and everyone who did have a third feels that their lives are fuller and better for it." For all the parents who feel this way, however, many decide they can't afford to pursue a larger family. For the Connecticut mom, "cost did, sadly, factor into the equation." But if the cost of a third child really is $3,830 a year or a little over $10 a day, then this would seem to be less of an obstacle than we think—unless the plunging costs reflect sacrifices that thoughtful parents wouldn't be willing to make.

AMORTIZING THE COST

So why do the marginal costs of children fall? Some economies of scale are pretty obvious, because you amortize the cost of purchases (a crib, a stroller, a high chair) over all the children. We bought very few baby outfits for Sam and instead have gone "shopping" every few months in Jasper's closet. Toys also get a new life with each new child who plays with them. What a younger child loses in newness, she gains in a collection of Legos that's been augmented by her older brothers' and sisters' Christmas and birthday gifts for years. You already have the swing set and tricycle, and unless one of them falls victim to a natural disaster or a rogue vehicle backing into it, you won't need to buy another.

Food can be bought in bulk—sometimes really in bulk. Tammy Metz of Pueblo, Colorado, a mother of nine, has a farmer acquaintance who "gave us a good deal on half a cow," she reports, enough to fill a freezer with beef. Jumbo packages of laundry detergent, cereal, and shampoo are often cheaper by the ounce than smaller packages. Smaller families may waste food that goes bad when you open a package and don't finish it; larger families have quicker turnover and of necessity wind up planning meals with this in mind. The savings are sometimes incredible. Mary Ostyn, of Nampa, Idaho, who has 10 kids (8 still at home), says she spends about $175 per week, or $700–$800 per month, on her family's food. She strategizes to hold herself to just two grocery store trips per week. "Once you get the system streamlined, it doesn't have to take forever," she says. She actually uses the 5-pound bags of grated cheese she buys at Costco that many of us let mold.

Basic transportation costs can fall, too. Once you've bought a minivan, which many families with two kids have done, sticking another kid in there doesn't cost anything. And you may not even have to buy that much car; enterprising parents have posted photos online of backseats featuring three car seats, latched straight across. It doesn't look comfortable, but it's doable.

For some families, child-care costs might also fall into the economies of scale category. Many Motherlode readers assumed the cost of child care for three young kids would be so prohibitive that one parent would have to stay home, though they differed on whether this was a cost savings (no day-care bills) or an expense (forgone earnings by the stay-at-home parent). But this calculation depends on what your cost structure looks like. In our case, we'd already taken the plunge to hiring a nanny with the second kid, so having a third added few immediate costs in this regard and in fact lowered the per child cost by quite a bit, though obviously adding a third kid restarted the clock on how many years we'd need full-time care before everyone was in school.

Some health-care costs also fall. In general, family insurance plans charge a certain rate to insure all adults and children in a family—a certain high rate, to be sure, but no higher for three kids than two. Co-pays for doctors' visits and prescriptions will add up faster with more children, but some insurance plans also have an out-of-pocket yearly maximum, which is the same no matter how many kids you have. In general, any service provider or attraction that offers a family plan is going to be cheaper per person for a large family than a smaller one. "Zoos and museums are great because they usually have family passes, and don't charge more if you have eight kids or have three," says Mary Ostyn. Some orthodontists, preschools, and even shoe stores offer discounts for multiple kids, thus lowering the marginal costs of each additional foot shod.

WHAT DO CHILDREN REQUIRE?

These economies of scale lead to lower marginal costs. But efficiencies alone don't account for the entire decline. Most people don't get raises when they bring another kid home from the hospital. Parents with three kids may spend less per kid not because they become better about money, but because they don't have the slack in their budget to spend more. In other words, there have to be lifestyle changes. From conversations with mega-families, I've found that many relish this reality. Large families have a definite countercultural vibe to them, even if many subscribe to more traditional politics. There are a lot of "cultural expectations that are put on families," says Chris

Jeub, whose wife, Wendy, is homeschooling their brood. "We sort of buck that."

Some of these changes likely aren't a big deal, like having kids share bedrooms and bathrooms, which lowers the marginal cost of housing. In the Jeub family, the boys share a room, the girls are split between two, and Mom and Dad get their own unless there's a baby in there with them. Many larger families also don't go out to eat much. As Ostyn says, "a mom with six kids is more likely to cook at home rather than take the kids to McDonald's."

But other trade-offs give the upwardly mobile greater pause. Consider children's activities. In the same Motherlode post, Lisa Belkin shared a note from a mom of four who said her "primary financial frustration" was "not being able to let them try a lot of classes and activities. I think many middle-class families with one or two children take it for granted that their children can each participate in at least one extracurricular activity per semester or year, if they so desire. The only thing we've done this year is tae kwon do, and we had to switch off—my older daughter took last semester, and my older son will take classes this semester. We did soccer last year but can't afford to continue this year. One daughter would like to try some kind of dance, but we can't afford it as long as her brother is taking martial arts. We'd like them to start on piano at some point so they can at least read music, but that's not in the budget either." She noted that "I don't want to overschedule them, but I do feel frustrated that I can't give them a chance to try things out and see where their talents might lie."

Lessons during the school year will add up fast, as will summer camps, both the arts and crafts and s'mores variety, but also academic camps for middle and high school students, which can expose them to more challenging work or original research projects. And then there's the matter of getting kids to all these places. Ballet lessons and soccer practice consume a lot of parents' time. "With one child, you may think nothing of a kid being in four different activities," says Mary Ostyn. "When you have five, six, or more kids, it would make you batty to have that many."

Larger families also change their expectations of where they can go. A $250 plane ticket to visit Grandma turns into a $1,500 ordeal if there are six of you. If you have family overseas, that will be even more expensive. Passport fees alone for multiple kids add up. So you start to stay local. The Ostyns go camping in the mountains, or rent a beach house off-season where they can stash everyone. Hotels are not only expensive, they often have rules about how many people can stay in each room.

And finally, there is the biggie: college. Most of the larger families I have interviewed do not intend to pay for college for their children (or private schools when their kids are younger). As Ostyn puts it, "our input into their college is to prepare them as well as possible for college and they can find ways to afford college on their own if they choose to go." She's done a good job on this front; two of her children have been National Merit Scholars, and all four of her oldest were eligible for scholarships due to high test scores, "which helped a lot with their college expenses," she says. Chris Jeub calls paying for college "a cultural expectation that parents don't really need to carry." It is an expectation with a hefty price tag. One Motherlode reader from Rochester, New York, wrote that "We have four ranging from 2–14. Taking the private colleges my wife and I attended as a base, the average increase for 4 tuitions is $43K per year, ignoring the underlying costs of $850K. That kind of number is beyond the means of the vast majority of parents to ever save."

So does any of this matter? A small proportion of families can spend as many resources on three or four kids as they would on two. If the kids all want to do four activities that require them to be at different places at the same time, then you just hire more people to drive them around. But for many people, more kids would seem to mean more trade-offs. This is what economist (and Nobel laureate) Gary Becker famously argued in his studies of the economics of the family. When there are more kids, families face a quality-quantity trade-off. Each child will be of lower "quality" because parents won't be able to feed and educate each one as well. This would seem to be more the case in developing countries without social safety nets or free schools, though fascinatingly, some research has shown that a reduction in fertility in poor communities doesn't necessarily lead to differences in height or weight or school enrollment, and that children in slightly larger families are not necessarily any worse off than children in smaller ones. Still, some trade-offs are inevitable, and so parents who do have a choice with their fertility need to weigh these matters. Are activities necessary? Is travel edifying? Does having parents who can contribute to your college education give you a leg up in life?

There are good arguments either way. Once I waded past the Motherlode comments claiming my third child would destroy the planet, I discovered that many readers had thought quite a bit about these trade-offs. As one wrote, "My husband and I absolutely based our decision to stop at two on not wanting to 'change our expectations' . . . We were both raised in financially tight (bigger) families, as in all our basic needs were met but there was nothing left over for experiences, activities or trips." As a social worker and a soldier, this mother wrote, "We are slightly more comfortable than our parents and have been able to give a wealth of experiences to our older son (and soon the younger when he can enjoy them) while also putting some away for both children's college expenses." This family thought about having a third child but realized it would require them to change their lifestyle. Their "fun savings" would be redeployed to other things. Their day-care costs would go up. So they decided to remain a party of four.

The desire to give children a wealth of experiences figured into many comments, with a big number of readers raising the question of nurturing children's potential. If you believe your child might someday become a world-class musician or athlete, then yes, it does matter whether you expose him to lessons as soon as possible. If you don't, given how competitive our globalized economy has become, you are likely precluding this possibility, because among the 7 billion people on this planet, others have started their kids on instruments and sports quite young. Tiger Woods was playing golf as a preschooler; if anything, the world will be more competitive in 2030 than it is now.

Even if you don't think your child is a prodigy, admission to highly selective colleges often hinges on having some other demonstrated ability beyond academics—athletically, musically, or otherwise. Not all kids whose parents pay for hockey lessons and leagues get recruited for college teams, but there are very few recruited athletes who didn't have exposure to good coaches and competitions early on. Likewise, special summer activities can help kids stand out. A growing number of research programs for high school students give kids both a chance to feed their minds and the means to enter the burgeoning array of contests (like the Intel Science Talent Search, or the Davidson Fellows program) that reward children for independent work. Sending three teens off to programs where they'll discover new elements of the periodic table is just going to be more expensive than sending one or two.

On the other hand, if you ask parents why they enroll their children in activities, they mention benefits such as learning teamwork, appreciating art and music, getting exercise, and heading off boredom so the kids don't get into trouble. Viewed in this light, one could argue that larger families don't have as much of a need for activities. As Tammy Metz notes, in her home "there is always someone to play with." If you have six kids, they will learn teamwork as they gang up against you, and if you have enough kids, they could probably just form their own sports team. As for music appreciation, rather than pursuing an individual instrumental career, kids can join a church or school choir or school orchestra, and pass down instruments as the older children abandon them. With athletics, we might be better off as a society if kids spent more time learning low-cost sports they can do by themselves their whole lives (running, biking, swimming) rather than team sports such as hockey, which they're unlikely to do often enough to stay in shape as adults.

Travel, likewise, may be a matter of taste. Camping is not inherently less fun than flying to Disney World. If kids are already stimulated by having multiple playmates at home, even going to the library can be exciting. "It's all about your perspective on what fun is," says Metz. You can ask far-flung family members to visit you. Having flown to Germany with Jasper when he was 19 months old, I can't say I'm eager to attempt more long plane flights with my little ones until they're not little ones, or until Lufthansa invents a special section for old German men who keep walking back to shake their fists at parents, as if they want their children to be crying. Kids may be just as happy to be shipped to Grandma's while the parents travel—a plan that may not be any more expensive than when you were newlyweds.

In my mind, out of all these experiences, college poses the biggest question. I know that paying for college was not easy for my parents. I think it was a good investment, because Princeton has opened many doors for me. I would like to be able to pay for my kids to go to college wherever they would like to go, and I'm sure many other parents feel the same way.

But what if my kids, with that idea in mind, decide they want to go somewhere that is expensive but not as beneficial to one's career as Princeton? Some expensive schools have fairly dismal graduation rates despite the quality of the students they admit. A recent American Enterprise Institute analysis of schools, grouped by selectivity, listed several top offenders among the elite: the New School charges

$31,940 yet posts a graduation rate of 61 percent. Bennington College ($36,800) graduates only 57 percent of students in six years. Tulane ($36,610) graduates 76 percent, which sounds good until you realize that schools that are similarly difficult to get into, such as the University of Notre Dame, graduate 95 percent of those who attend.

There is also the question of moral hazard. If my kids know I'll pay for them to go to college, will they work as hard for the good grades that might attract merit scholarships? Will they be willing to work part-time jobs? While the sticker prices on some elite schools sound atrocious, affording a school like Princeton or Harvard has actually gotten more doable for a student paying her own way in the past few years, rather than less. If your family earns up to $180,000 a year, Harvard now charges roughly 10 percent of income. So if your family earns $100,000, Harvard will cost $10,000, or $40,000 for four years (plus a small student contribution). A young person could probably earn $5,000–$7,500 a year during each of those four years, and take out $20,000 in loans. A $20,000 student debt is not ideal for starting life, but it's also roughly average these days.

Harvard chose the 10 percent number to make its tuition (for upper-middle-income families) roughly comparable with that of flagship state schools, which are not only great bargains but can also be good for one's career. The *Wall Street Journal* publishes an annual list of the top schools where corporate recruiters like to hire. Penn State topped the list in 2010. Next? Texas A&M, where my husband went on a scholarship. One data point does not make a theorem, but he does outearn me, which may be why he's a little less concerned about the "paying Ivy League tuition" goal than I am.

Nonetheless, it is human nature—Darwinian, even—to want to give our offspring any advantages we can. We live in a competitive, globalized world, and the popularity of activities and camps and college prep workshops stems not only from a desire to help our children but also a worry that something has changed in our economy. We wonder if our kids will have the same standard of living we've had even if they work harder than we ever had to. Once upon a time, after high school, you walked down to the local factory and got a job. Your only competition was your neighbors. We know this is no longer true, but we are still searching for something that will guarantee our children a good life. Is it a test prep course? The right internship? Some 70 percent of high school graduates now enroll in college, most in the hopes of achieving an upper-middle-class income. But this is becoming mathematically impossible. We cannot all earn more than average. When I started writing this chapter, popular culture had become completely dominated by conversations about "Tiger mothers." Yale Law School professor Amy Chua's memoir of her demanding parenting, *The Battle Hymn of the Tiger Mother*, fanned fears that somehow those of us who lean a bit to the squishy side just aren't doing enough to guarantee our children's success.

Those worries are magnified by all the tales from this latest recession of young people with impressive educations who still can't get jobs. One cringing moment for me was interviewing a young lady who graduated with honors from Amherst and who'd recently beaten out hundreds of other candidates for a job walking dogs. In a world like that, it's easy to hope that investing more resources in fewer children will somehow help them achieve the lives they (or we?) want.

But what I find most intriguing about larger families is that many seem to accept, even if their politics sometimes points them differently, that all this is grasping at straws. Not much we consciously do as parents has any long-term effect on the adult success of our children. Studies of adoption, identical vs. fraternal twins, and even twins raised apart are increasingly finding how limited parental effects beyond our genes really are. Bryan Caplan's 2011 book, *Selfish Reasons to Have More Kids*, lists these studies by the score—all of which create a drumbeat for the notion that while parents can change things in the short run, in the long run, we tend to have the greatest effect within that moment of conception. "Instead of thinking of children as lumps of clay for parents to mold, we should think of them as plastic that flexes in response to pressure—and pops back to its original shape once the pressure is released," he writes. Within the norms for middle-class households, the flash cards don't matter. The trips don't matter. The lessons don't matter except for the tiny number of people who will become professionals in artistic or sports fields, and even then, since there's such a winner-take-all effect, these investments may not have a positive effect on future outcomes.

Even seemingly big things don't matter. Consider that oft-repeated maxim that "it's best if one parent stays home with the children." While occasional studies find one statistically significant result—which then gets blasted into headlines—the overall volume of literature comes out as a wash on this question. Why? Because kids are complicated creatures. At-home mothers spend a bit more time playing with their kids. But CDC research has found that young children at home with a parent are also more likely to watch television for more than two hours per day, compared to kids in day-care centers. People are a sum of too many variables to know that particular parental decisions will lead to certain future outcomes. Unless you have a trust fund that will support your children forever, there is nothing you can do to guarantee their financial stability, and even a trust fund won't guarantee them success or happiness in life. Probably the best thing we can do for our kids, psychologically, is to create happy homes, not given to extremes, where the parents are content with their choices. The best thing we can do for our kids, economically, is to teach them to be entrepreneurial. A big chunk of this is helping them develop an internal locus of control—that is, the belief that they are responsible for making their way in the world. No one is going to hand them a job or an opportunity. They will have to go seek it out.

I don't know if such a belief is more or less likely in large families.

But I do know there are nonfinancial benefits to having more people around for building social ties, a factor that is strongly correlated with happiness. My mother-in-law's four children and growing collection of grandchildren—not to mention her own siblings—keep her busy enough that you have to get on her schedule in advance if you want a babysitter during peak times. As a Motherlode commenter wrote, in large families, "rarely is one sibling isolated . . . as another is likely to take his or her side or simply support the right to disagree . . . When the children have their own children, the younger generation [has] plenty of aunts and uncles who are diverse in interests and professions to serve as role models as well as some models of bad decisions to avoid." A child might never get a new bike, but his older siblings will teach him to ride. Each child might get less parental time but gets more time with siblings.

"So was it worth it?" one Motherlode reader asked of her larger family. "I have six people in this world who share the battle wounds of growing up in a big family. Six people who understand me. Six people to help me through the roughest times in my life that are guaranteed to come. Six people to share burdens with. . . . Sure my childhood was crowded, but that was 18 years. I have my whole adulthood ahead of me and I'll always be one of seven . . . Maybe it might not have made a difference had I just had one other sibling. I'll never know. But I do know that the knowledge that I'm not going through life alone was worth all the crowdedness, unfairness, constant sharing [and] lack of privacy that I experienced as a kid."

This was certainly what I was hoping with welcoming a third child into the world. Plus, given what awesome little people my sons are turning out to be, the odds seem good that my daughter will make my life richer as well. And if she'll be relatively cheap, so much the better. I always like a bargain.

CHAPTER 7

The Chicken Mystique

Growing up, I was quite the student of survivalist literature. I was especially intrigued by *The Boxcar Children*, the midcentury book series whose first installment told the story of how some runaway kids lived off their wits and little else. They furnished the abandoned railcar they chose as their home with items scrounged from junk piles. The older children worked odd jobs for money, stretching their pennies as far as possible, but the scene I remember best from the first book involved 14-year-old Henry feeding his siblings produce salvaged from a doctor's garden.

I've long pondered why I—and millions of other children—enjoyed that story and others like it. Some of you may have been obsessed with the *Little House on the Prairie* series and the tales of Laura Ingalls's family building a sod house and stockpiling their harvests for winter. In these literary worlds, people did not use cash to obtain most of the things they needed. A few cents changed hands at the store for cloth or salt, but on the whole it was almost unnecessary for a full life. Our heroes survived on their creativity and the generosity of their neighbors. They made furniture, soap, and clothes themselves, thus living in a greener fashion than those of us who drive out of our way to buy pricey plant-based detergent at specialty stores could imagine. In a complex world, perhaps we are intrigued by their simple self-reliance.

Regardless, as the banking system went into paroxysms recently and as many of us seek to live a truly low-impact life, this pioneer mind-set is back in vogue. We celebrate a do-it-yourself impulse that tries to separate the household, on the margins, from the larger economy. Retro homesteading is hip to the point where Ree Drummond's blog of rustic photos and recipes, The Pioneer Woman, draws millions of visitors a month. Edible gardening is such an eminent social movement that it has invaded the White House lawn. Swapping and bartering and other forms of cashless transactions are catching on, aided by technology that can match people who have extra stuff with those who want the surplus. On the extremes, this movement is chronicled in Shannon Hayes's *Radical Homemakers*, a 2010 manifesto for women (and/or men) to return to home and hearth and create a form of homemaking more meaningful than the chauffeuring and shopping Betty Friedan lamented in *The Feminine Mystique*. The idea is that households can thrive on one—or even fewer—incomes if the homemaker learns old-fashioned skills such as small-scale farming, canning, animal husbandry, sewing, home repair, and so forth. The household goes from being part of the "extractive economy" with its environmental and moral compromises to the production economy, achieving deeper meaning through creative work than many people experience commuting to a job, buying stuff, and spending their leisure time watching TV. The happiest people don't *need* to get and spend. They achieve fulfillment via self-sufficiency and nurturing their connection with the earth.

Judging by the number of my friends now raising chickens in their backyards, it's a seductive argument. Even if most of us won't go all the way toward renouncing the cash economy, we view this old-fashioned do-it-yourself impulse as more meaningful than other fun hobbies, either because it's green or because it seems like a step up the frugal ladder from mere coupon clipping. Think of all the money you save by producing your own organic eggs, growing your own tomatoes, and sewing your own clothes! The made-from-scratch economy seems to be the epitome of laughing at the Joneses. It means discovering a freedom and self-determined wealth that all the money in the world can't buy.

I do believe we should spend our time and money on things that make us happy. For many people, chickens, farming, tinkering, and the like do just that. But this widespread adoption of what I call the "chicken mystique"—the near-evangelical belief that we will all find intrinsic meaning in green, cashless living just as Friedan's housewives were supposed to find meaning in waxing their floors—requires certain assumptions about the value of time, money, and work. As intriguing as I find *The Boxcar Children*, the more I think about these assumptions, the more I worry that they have a downside, particularly in the context of women's changing roles. There are ways to use money to promote sustainable living without shunning the efficiencies gleaned from the larger modern economy. You can live a green and happy life and still focus your talents on spheres beyond the domestic—such as running a blog on pioneer living that generates a seven-figure revenue per year, something the Ingalls family of *Little House on the Prairie* fame would have been thrilled to be able to do. As part of the grand search for meaning and happiness, there are plenty of reasons not to live as if it's 1870 or the Great Depression, and plenty of reasons to remember the opportunity cost of time in our attempts to be fiscally smart.

A CLUCKING TREND

Whenever I start writing about a new topic, I cajole readers on my blog or on Facebook to help me find "real people" who could illustrate the story. Sometimes this is like pulling teeth. Not so with chicken raising. Approximately five minutes after I posted a query asking if anyone knew someone who kept a coop, someone who could give me insights into the practice, I got dozens of leads to people who, at first glance, didn't seem particularly agrarian. Take the case of Susan Bredimus of Tempe, Arizona. She works for a company owned by Aetna, authorizing mental health care services. She "never would have thought of having chickens," but when her mother and husband died within a short time of each other, "my life literally came to a screeching halt." Looking for something to distract herself, she brought home a few chicks. "When I started it was more therapeutic," she says. "Then I fell in love with them. They're adorable." Now she keeps six chickens in her backyard, where they bask in the desert sun or lounge under her orange trees. They are a well-pampered brood. Bredimus has been known to play the chicks Native American flute music to relax them, and on Thanksgiving she closes the curtains so they won't suffer the trauma of seeing her stuff a turkey. With such loving care, the chickens each produce an egg a day year-round.

The reasons people give for raising chickens are as varied as the owners. In an age of salmonella scares and factory farming, some people want to know where their food is coming from. Or they just consider fresh, homegrown food to be better ("I can't even go out to breakfast anymore because the eggs don't taste good," Bredimus says). Some want to tread lightly on and feel closer to the earth, and others want to shell out less at the grocery store. Bridget Lorenz of Anoka, Minnesota, notes that when you figure in feed, her family's eggs cost about 15 cents apiece. "We don't save money compared to the 99-cent-per-dozen eggs, but we do save compared to organic eggs," she says, which can run $4 a dozen for the free-range variety. Some people go all out, indulging their chickens the way they'd indulge any other pet. The March 2011 issue of *Martha Stewart Living* features veterinarian and horse breeder Dede McGehee's sprawling Kentucky farm where "the gardener had planned on a no-frills coop for the birds until designer Deborah Ludorf drew a miniature version of the home being built for McGehee," writer Susan Heeger explains. Net result: a henhouse that looks like a country estate you'd see in, well, *Martha Stewart Living.* Jen Boulden, a green business entrepreneur who sold her e-mail newsletter, Ideal Bite, to the Walt Disney Company in 2008, raises chickens in her backyard in Bozeman, Montana. "It's kind of relaxing, like watching goldfish, watching all these chickens bobble around your yard, eating little bugs from the grass, snatching up mosquitos from the air, and even jumping into your big potted plants to make a nest," she says. She splits her time between Bozeman and Los Angeles, and plans to make chickens a part of her LA lifestyle as well.

The chickens are just the most photogenic part of this larger societal interest in small-scale farming. Even people who don't want to raise animals can follow Michelle Obama's lead and grow their own vegetables—on a windowsill if necessary—and many do. Sometimes this is for financial reasons, sometimes for philosophical reasons, sometimes for entertainment, and sometimes for all three. In 2009 as the economy cratered, gardening supply company W. Atlee Burpee & Co. reported a massive spike in vegetable seed sales. Barbara Kingsolver made such agrarian practices sound enticing with her 2007 book, *Animal, Vegetable, Miracle*, chronicling a year spent eating food mostly grown on her own farm or nearby. She raised her own turkeys. She canned her own tomatoes. She grew her own pumpkins and lamented that Thanksgiving recipes all listed pumpkin as the first ingredient in the form of a 15-ounce can. Michael Pollan's food writing likewise cajoles people to get out of the grocery store, where much of the merchandise springs from the industrial food system, and the urban renewal movement has people starting farms in vacant lots from Philadelphia to Detroit. Rich Awn, the host of Green Air, which airs on CBS affiliate radio stations nationwide, lives in Greenpoint, Brooklyn, and farms his postage-stamp-sized backyard. This little spot of earth produces enough for him to "eat a tomato for lunch every day" and still have plenty left over to give to his neighbors. "I really enjoy growing stuff and seeing the pace of life—how things go from seeds to something you can eat," he says.

Awn also forages a bit, another *Boxcar Children*-esque technique people are reviving to obtain food without patronizing the supermarket. Rebecca Lerner, a 20-something journalist who lives in Portland, Oregon, has conducted a few experiments with scrounging for wild-food sources in the modern world. Indigenous people used to live in Portland the same way, so she figured it was doable. Unfortunately, her first attempt in May 2009 didn't work out well. "It's really not that simple," she told me. "You really do have to plan." A human being needs a tremendous volume of food when just eating greens, which is why she's come to suspect that indigenous hunter-gatherers relied on their communities, with people specializing in certain foods. They also maintained root cellars. "They were really into storage," she says. Seasons matter; "you can't just live on what's there in any given season." They gathered nuts and fruits and preserved them. Not knowing this the first time around, she tried to live off the land for a week and didn't quite make it. "I was basically just winging it, eating dandelion, chickweed, eating burdock root, thistle roots, all of which have very few calories, and I was spending hours walking around looking for stuff and had to dig it up. It became very exhausting and time consuming and I was basically getting salad and tea." A few days in, she was faint and seeing spots and called it quits.

But she did her research and tried again in November 2009, casting a broader net, incorporating black walnuts, chestnuts, hazelnuts, wapato (a tuber sometimes called "Indian potato"), and wild mushrooms. She also asked for help from friends and ate reasonably well. She believes that "foraging is something that ties us into why we're on earth—it gives us a strong connection to the earth in a way that abstract ideas of moralizing about the environment, or even the beauty of the forest, can't do." After we talked, she e-mailed me that roadkill was also "a great foraged cash-free food resource," especially in colder climates. "In the winter months, when it's below freezing outside, it's safe to eat, and some people do. I do know people in Portland who eat roadkill, but we have a lot less of it out here, and it's also not quite as safe because it's a warmer climate. I consider it 'hunted by car.'" While eating roadkill sounds extreme to most of us (and the legality of collecting it for eating varies widely by jurisdiction), plenty of people hunt and fish, both for fun and as a way to supplement their food budgets. A few animals go a long way. A single buck (male deer, for the uninitiated) could yield close to 70 pounds of meat, or 140 eight-ounce servings. People in Alaska can fill whole freezers with a fraction of a moose.

Producing or finding one's own food can complement a broad range of activities that avoid entanglement with the monetary economy. Take swapping. Trading goods for other goods is an ancient practice, though it's long suffered from the difficulty of producing a "dual coincidence of wants." Just because you have a cow to trade doesn't mean you want what the other guy has on offer, so you're highly likely to suffer from "dual wants of coincidence." But modern technology makes swapping goods, services, or experiences more feasible. The Web site Couchsurfing.org, for instance, helps people who want to travel cheaply and share their stories match up with people who want company and have couches to share. I recently met a writer and father named Matthew Winkler who homeschooled his son in sixth grade by taking him couch surfing (and skateboarding) in all 50 states. Chronicled on his Web site 50skatekid.com, the whole adventure took just a few thousand bucks. Per the Radical Homemaking idea, this experiment in stepping partially outside the cash economy let Winkler's family live quite well on one income (his wife's) and produce memories Winkler and his son will savor their whole lives.

Other swapping sites traffic in more traditional goods. Swap.com uses an algorithm to produce dual coincidences of wants from thousands of users, who can then exchange their used books and DVDs for other used books and DVDs, without having to purchase these items new. Likewise, thredUP.com lets parents exchange boxes of used children's clothes. Carly Fauth, who now works for thredUP and is the mom of a one-year-old boy, reports that "swapping was something I never really thought about, but it's such a great concept for younger kids. I was spending so much money on clothes for my son. I have not bought him one thing in the past eight months. It's saved me a ton of money." This could be a way to lower the marginal cost of kids, even if you have only one.

Some folks also try to avoid monetary entanglement by bartering for services. If done legally, this doesn't remove cash from the equation. According to the IRS, both parties in a bartering transaction are supposed to report the fair market value of services they received as income, and then pay taxes on this amount. I imagine, however, that this is one of the most flouted tax laws on the books, as the IRS isn't exactly deploying auditors to check if neighbors are trading off babysitting for interior design services.

Regardless, if a household did use all these techniques, you can see how someone might live on a very low income. Rich Awn generates enough cash each month to pay his rent by renting out his extra bedroom, doing the occasional real estate deal, and various other jobs. But by foraging, farming, and bartering the kombucha he brews, he "tries to live outside the money economy as much as I can" as he trades his fermented beverage for different goods and services.

"Money makes people weird," he says. "It makes people greedy, makes them act differently. Every venture I've gotten involved in, as soon as money's on the table, everybody wants some of it." *Radical Homemakers* is full of tales of families living (albeit sometimes without health insurance for the grown-ups) on $30,000 a year or less by producing their own food, sewing their own clothes, and bartering for what they need. "Money becomes a marginal chit when a family can cultivate self-reliance and community interdependence," writes Shannon Hayes. "Mainstream Americans have lost the simple domestic skills that would enable them to live an ecologically sensible life with a modest or low income."

BUYING TIME

Perhaps because I was so fascinated by *The Boxcar Children* and *Little House on the Prairie*, I did learn many of these domestic skills myself. As a child, I once built my own dollhouse. My seventh grade home economics teacher claimed I'd done the best button sewing job she'd ever seen. I have boiled chicken bones to make soup stock, learned to cook in bulk for leftovers, used my sewing skills to alter thrift store finds, and lived without a car in a situation when it would have been a lot easier to have one. Unlike many DIYers, I haven't always done these things just for fun; having these skills let me live on less than $1,000 a month during a time in my life when I thought that would be prudent. As a writer, you never plan on being well compensated. My *Boxcar Children* mentality definitely helped me realize, when I was younger, that I could live a reasonable life without a regular job. And so, I can see the appeal of the chicken mystique, not just as a hobby but as a lifestyle. Some homemaking practices are fun because you can do them with family; my children, for instance, planted some vegetables with their grandmother in our backyard. My hope is that the experience will induce them to sample more items from this food group, though unlike Kingsolver, I know better than to expect animals, vegetables, *and* miracles.

But the rise of the chicken mystique raises broader questions of what money is and does, and how we assign value—questions I wasn't really pondering when I was 23, had fewer demands on my time, and could get away with carrying a cheap health insurance policy that I now realize would have been problematic had anything gone wrong.

For some do-it-yourselfers, money is to be avoided whenever possible because of what it stands for. Devotees of the chicken mystique quote Thoreau that "the cost of a thing is the amount of what I will call life which is required to be exchanged for it, immediately or in the long run." If you believe Awn, money makes people weird. It pushes us to consign ourselves to wage slavery, though this is obviously a value we're assigning to it, rather than something inherent in these coins and pieces of paper. On their own, they are as innocuous as buttons and greeting cards.

Indeed, if you think about it, currency is a brilliant invention, to convey such meaning in easily minted things. Humans started using metal objects as money as long ago as 5000 B.C., and China has been using paper money for more than a thousand years. The United States got onboard during the Civil War. Congress created a national banking system in 1865 and levied a tax on state currencies, basically making them unprofitable and leading to one national—albeit wildly fluctuating—currency. The Federal Reserve Act of 1913 created an authority (the Federal Reserve) to even all this out. The Fed has its critics, but life is certainly easier with a portable, national, relatively stable currency. Here in the United States, people even post transparent prices for everything! As I've learned from travels in Morocco and elsewhere, haggling can be exhausting. Even if, as Awn says, money makes people greedy, it is an extremely efficient way of allocating resources. Rather than carting around gallons of kombucha, you bring a nice, thin wallet—and these days, often a credit or debit card rather than wads of cash. Indeed, money is so efficient that when you choose not to use it, and try to step outside the monetary economy, you must pay with something else: time.

The problem with the chicken mystique is that time has a cost, too. And I've found that often, time is more valuable than the money saved—or even the short-term satisfaction gained by spending it. As Rebecca Lerner notes of foraging, "it's not free. It's just moneyless."

She has spent quite a bit of time pondering the question of whether foraging saves her money or not, and her thoughts have gone back and forth. Even when she foraged effectively, her gathering of plants, nuts, fruits, and berries took hours every day. "Processing acorns is a really tremendously time-consuming experience," she tells me. You harvest the acorns, crack the shells and dry them, then immerse them in water to get the bitter tannins out of them, dry them again, and then pound them into flour before they're usable. This process takes days. No matter what you're earning, you're probably not going to come out ahead when you consider the cost of time. "At the moment I would consider myself broke," Lerner says, but as a city dweller she has still not found foraging to be viable as an exclusive source of calories. She considers it more as a supplement—something she's continued writing about at her blog, FirstWays.com. "It kind of gives me comfort," she says, to walk down a street and see weeds because she thinks "oh, I could put that in my salad." She's expanded her range by posting Craigslist ads offering free weeding, by communicating with parks officials about invasive species they want removed, and by befriending neighbors with fecund yards. She also points out that cities could plant more fruit- and nut-bearing trees in public spaces if they wanted, and thus get us closer to the landscape America's indigenous people harvested.

But overall, the sheer time involved would give most of us pause.

Put it this way: even when they're only supplementing a diet, foragers can spend hours thinking about food. The best thing about using money to buy food from people who specialize in producing or procuring it is that we can use our brains to think about other things: science, industry, conquering Wii games, whatever. This is what made civilization possible.

Farming likewise requires hours to till the soil, plant, tend, and harvest. A commercial farm achieves economies of scale. A backyard farmer, less so. In the Great Depression, people had little choice. With fewer social supports, being an out-of-work breadwinner meant you were out of luck. And so our forebears stitched children's clothes out of feed sacks, starched their shirts in water they'd used to boil potatoes, patched together shards of soap because they couldn't afford a new bar, and ground corn for corn bread—all of which works fine unless, for instance, the crops don't come up. Then you get massive social upheavals: the "Okies," as in *The Grapes of Wrath*, moving to California, or Irish migrants fleeing the potato famine. While living on unemployment benefits and food stamps these days is tough, these social supports do allow people to stay in the cash economy—and are clearly more efficient than the subsistence farming people undertake of necessity in rural Asia or Africa (a close comparison to what some people in the United States lived through during the Depression, or what the Ingalls family thought of as normal). Anytime I'm tempted to romanticize small-scale farming, I remind myself that through history, many bright children, including my own grandfather for a time, had to stop going to school because their labor was required on family farms. The specialized economy may have its woes, but its cashless, agrarian precursor was responsible for squandering far more human capital.

Few would claim that America's social supports are generous, and so in theory backyard gardening can be a way to stretch the value of income transfers. But even so, it's not clear, if paid work is a remote option, that making one's own food helps much. A small batch of chickens might lay you two dozen eggs a week. Organic free-range eggs cost about $4 a dozen in the store. Regular eggs run closer to $1–$2. The federal minimum wage is $7.25 an hour. If you could clear $6 an hour, then your chicken work would have to take you less than 1.33 hours per week to be economical compared with buying organic—and that doesn't count the start-up costs, which are highly variable.

So how much time do these "cashless" activities take? Time-use researchers have discovered that people are quite bad at estimating how much time they spend on activities like caring for pets or pro-curing food, and the ranges I got from chicken devotees were all over the map. Bridget Lorenz reports that "it doesn't take much time, maybe five to ten minutes a day, to feed, water, collect the eggs, wash them, and date them. Then once a week (sometimes every other week) twenty to thirty minutes to clean out the coop." Sometimes this labor is pleasant and sometimes it isn't. "It's exciting and cute to see my kids excited to collect eggs and playing with the chicks last spring," Lorenz says. "It's not so fantastic to have to drag myself out of the house on a freezing Saturday morning to take them water or scoop out the stinking straw from the coop." Stephanie Jaquez Miller estimates that her family spends eight hours a week on chicken up-keep. "We average four eggs a day in the winter but we get twelve a day in the spring and summer," she says. Even so, at $4 a dozen, an hour a day works from a time vs. money perspective only if you value your time at nothing.

Some people believe the convenience and money-saving factor of modern swapping is oversold, too. Calee Lee, a mom of two small kids, tells me that "I used thredUP once, but I found that I hated the chore of mailing a box." Better to ask people for clothes as gifts, she decided, and give away her old clothes without involving the postal service. Even bartering can be problematic, leaving aside the issue of paying taxes on the equivalent income (which removes any monetary advantage whatsoever). "I experimented with bartering graphic design and printing services for house cleaners," Lee says, "but I found that when real money wasn't involved—even if I was providing business cards that were 'worth' much more than one cleaning—people were much less likely to show up."

So does this matter that cashless living costs a lot of time? My survivalist literature fetish notwithstanding, and understanding that knitting and chicken raising can be enjoyable activities in their own right, I now know it does to me. Many of us could make more money if we decided that was a family priority. None of us can make more time. We all have 168 hours a week, and no one can devote more time to anything than that. One of my big discoveries as my life has become busier is that—once I've cut out the obvious time wasters of TV and random Web surfing—money can buy back some of those 168 hours from chores, so those hours can be redeployed to things that I find more meaningful. Topping the meaningful list for me are what I consider my core competencies: nurturing my family, writing books and articles that interest me, maintaining my own health (largely through running and getting adequate sleep), and participating in carefully chosen volunteer activities. It is not that I don't find growing one's own food and sewing one's own clothes meaningful, it's that I know these things are less meaningful to me than my core competencies. Like dollars, time spent on one thing is time not spent on something else. Time spent feeding chickens is time I'm not writing about people who do such things. Time spent canning and preserving is time I'm not running or volunteering. In theory, pioneer-style farming and food chores can be done with one's children, but when you have little ones, these tasks often wind up being done with even less efficiency than they would normally involve. Chances are, you'll be at the store buying tomatoes because your preschooler "harvested" the crop in your garden prematurely. You can be mad about that, or you can be grateful that the modern economy lets us have tomatoes when we want them *and* less stressful interactions with our kids.

Of course, the reason I choose the side of the equation I do is that I *enjoy* all my core competencies, including my paid work. The crux of the chicken mystique is that spending time on producing one's own food or other goods is more enjoyable than other things one could do to earn an equivalent amount of money—or if not more enjoyable, is at least more meaningful in the same way that raising children is more meaningful than having extra leisure time, even though watching TV is more fun than changing diapers. For some people this chicken mystique equation may be true. Bridget Lorenz notes that "Since I grew up with animals on a farm I wanted my kids to have a similar experience of taking care of animals and being connected to where their food comes from . . . They understand the life cycle of chickens and that food doesn't come from the grocery store but that there are people that work very hard and animals that give their lives so that we can eat. It's part of teaching them to be grateful and mindful."

I am a big fan of being grateful and mindful. But one can learn about animals and food and hard work in many ways, and likewise, one can derive meaning from many things in life—including paid work. A key complication with the chicken mystique, at least in its extreme forms, is that not all jobs are meaningless drains on one's time, a form of drudgery wise women should do anything they can to minimize or avoid. Even some proponents of the chicken mystique concede this. As Shannon Hayes writes, "not all careers are soul-sucking ventures (if they were, I wouldn't be investing so much time in writing this book)." And not all homemaking is soul-building. Just as Betty Friedan found in *The Feminine Mystique*, we become full people when we do things to change the world. The "problem that has no name," as Friedan called it, was that housework has never been particularly fulfilling to most people beyond the folks who decide to start their own cleaning businesses. You can dress it up all you want with fancy gadgets, but vacuuming a rug is still just vacuuming a rug . . . unless you imbue it with some larger purpose. This is what the chicken mystique offers people. You're not just making dinner, you're making the world greener by growing dinner! You're not just making your own laundry soap and thereby saving cash at the store, you're reducing your carbon footprint and saving the world! Radical Home-makers, Hayes writes, don't just stay home. They lead campaigns to change the laws to allow chicken raising in urban areas, or they pres-sure corporations to change their practices. Ideally, each home would be "the center for social change, the starting point from which a bet-ter life would ripple out for everyone."

But here's a thought: all this raising chickens and sewing clothes is an inefficient way of getting at the concept of having a larger pur-pose and contributing financially. If you want a larger purpose, and want to contribute financially to your family, what's wrong with get-ting a job that does this? You'll make more progress on the green front running a utility than you will with your garden. You can make grand social change from within institutions: changing operations at a major apparel company to pay factory workers a living wage, de-signing curricula for a school system that encourages independent thought, acquiring books at a publishing house that advance ideas about social justice. But to do these things, you have to be part of the larger economy. You have to use your time and talents to conquer ex-isting institutions. That will be challenging, sure. But the results may be even more radical than one can achieve with backyard chickens.

CHANGING THE WORLD

I know that many people who dabble in edible gardening and chicken raising are doing it just for the sheer fun of it, not as a political statement or as anything else. That is fair enough. We should spend our time and resources on things that we enjoy. For some people this is gardening, for others it's genealogical research, for others it's playing the piano, and for some it's watching sports on TV. The question for many of us is, if we think our time is best spent working in jobs we love and nurturing our families and ourselves, rather than canning tomatoes, how can we still use our money in a sustainable way? If you view factory farms, mass-produced supermarket food, and many consumer goods as environmentally and morally compromised, then how can you still spend your money in ways that align with your values? Can you do this without losing the efficiencies of a market economy and the ability to deploy your talents as they would be best compensated?

My first thought is that being a mindful steward of your money is always a good approach. Why buy things you don't need or, if you think about it, want? In the long run, stuff tends to make us less happy than experiences, unless there is a clear path from that stuff to a happy memory, like reading *Little House on the Prairie* with your kids. If that stuff comes with mounds of wasteful packaging, that's an even better reason to think twice about bringing it into your life.

But broadly, the best approach seems to be to get to know your local economy. There are many reasons to do this, but the upside is that if you care about how things are produced, then you should get to know the people who produce them. This doesn't need to take much time. If you make two grocery shopping trips a week, make one to a supermarket and one to a farmers' market. Or get food delivered from sources you trust (such as Tim Will's Farmers Fresh

Market, mentioned in chapter 3, if you happen to live in the western North Carolina region). It's more expensive, but if you're working full-time in a job you genuinely enjoy, you'll likely have the cash to cover it. Buy clothes from designers who can tell you how they source their fabric; buy furniture from craftsmen who make it. That way these people can focus on what they do best, and you can focus on what you do best, paying each other with that convenient chit known as money. After all, money is just a tool, like fire. Some people misuse fire, and some people assign too much meaning to money—whether they love it or hate it. But like most tools, it's really just a more efficient and useful means toward whatever ends we desire. Even achieving happiness.

SHARING

CHAPTER 8

The Selfish Joy of Giving

Say you find a few bucks in your coat pocket. You debate whether to spend the money on yourself or give it away. Which do you think would make you happier?

For a 2008 paper published in *Science*, researchers Elizabeth Dunn, Lara Aknin, and Michael Norton ran an experiment to find out. They gave people either $5 or $20, and assigned them to two groups. One group was told to spend the money by 5 P.M. on themselves. The other had to spend the cash on someone else, either as a gift or by giving it to charity. The size of the windfall turned out not to matter, but those who gave the money away reported a significant uptick in happiness compared to where they started the day. The personal spending group did not.

Other studies appear to confirm this. For the same article, the researchers followed a group of employees who received an end-of-year profit-sharing bonus. They measured their happiness before receiving the bonus, and after. The only significant predictor of happiness at the second check-in was pro-social spending—what chunk of the bonus was spent on gifts or charitable donations. The researchers also did a broad survey of Americans, asking people how much they spent on bills and themselves, and how much they spent on others. Personal spending was unrelated to happiness, whereas pro-social spending was associated with significantly greater well-being.

Why would this be? It seems counterintuitive. Wouldn't buying a DVD for yourself make you happier than buying a DVD for someone else? If you buy a DVD for yourself, you get something tangible out of the deal and likely the pleasant experience of watching it. Indeed, when Dunn, Aknin, and Norton asked 109 students whether spending money on themselves or others would make them happier, a majority of students chose personal spending. But humans are social creatures and operate under a basic need to feel connected to other people, to feel part of something greater than themselves. Small gifts can satisfy that need in a way that personal spending does not. Given how much effort we spend pursuing happiness—buying sleeker cars and bigger rings—the fact that spending a mere $5 on someone else can boost one's mood suggests that we could save ourselves serious time merely by becoming more generous.

It's an intriguing idea. Of course, as we look at the intersection of money and happiness, it soon becomes apparent that there are many ways to give, some of which are more enjoyable than others. These subjective factors are not 100 percent rational. For instance, days after the fact, I still feel happy about giving a woman at the bus stop $5 when she asked for $1, just as the research in *Science* suggests. I'm more irked, however, by a clerk's loud (and management-forced) request at the drugstore counter that I donate to a diabetes-related nonprofit. This is true even though I have no idea what the bus stop lady did with my cash, whereas I'm sure the diabetes charity is impeccably managed. I'm not alone in this. In general, people find that giving is most fun when done in ways that allow us to establish direct connections with the people and projects we support.

Fortunately for those of us who feel this way, the nonprofit universe is changing to make personalized giving more possible than ever before, though—as with my preference for the bus stop lady vs. the diabetes collection—the rise of such philanthropy raises serious questions about whether giving should center on our own happiness. The answer, I believe, is a qualified yes. This touch of selfishness may be disconcerting in a field that's supposed to be about altruism, but when people can take charge of their own giving—feeling like philanthropists who have all the money in the world to give—they do more good in the long term than through more passive methods. If we view giving through the lens of happiness, this suggests a certain approach for giving money away that we'll cover at the end of the chapter. The goal is to discover how to wring the most joy out of each charitable buck, while maybe changing the world as well.

FAMILY-TO-FAMILY

One of the more exciting stories of the past two decades is how the nonprofit world—once seen as the genteel province of large, if staid players—has undergone a start-up revolution similar to the one that's swept the for-profit world. Today, people talk of social entrepreneurship. They strive for innovative business plans. Rather than simply seeking checks, people talk about how to keep donors engaged and how to spot a need and quickly meet it.

This is precisely what happened with a Westchester, New York–based nonprofit called Family-to-Family, which had its genesis with a disturbing 2002 newspaper article.

On September 29 of that year, I, and presumably thousands of other people, read a cover story in the *New York Times* about Pembroke, Illinois. In this small town a little over an hour from Chicago, "some still live in crumbling shacks with caked-dirt floors and no running water," reporter John W. Fountain wrote. "There are half a dozen liquor stores and scores of churches. But there is no bank. No supermarket. No police force. No barbershop. No gas station. No pharmacy." To illustrate the entrenched poverty of the place, he told the story of LaCheir Daniels, a single mom of five children living in a house with a kitchen floor that was caving in, a broken water heater, and nonfunctional windows. "A high school dropout, Ms. Daniels, who grew up in Pembroke, has worked sparingly in her 29 years, mostly at temporary factory jobs. Her monthly allotment of food stamps is $450 . . . She is able-bodied and willing to work, she says. But she has no transportation." Her mother, sister, and brother helped her with her $125/month rent, though not the four fathers of her five children, who "became ghosts when it came time to buy diapers and milk." The article ended with Daniels serving her children the lone meal of the day—pasta and neck bones. After the five kids ate, there was nothing left for her. And in the last week of the month, with her food stamp supply exhausted, there would be no more food for days unless they figured something out.

It was a powerful story, even though it raised as many questions as it answered. Why, with Chicago and all its jobs an hour away, would people stay in Pembroke? Why did some residents, when offered new homes, choose to stay in their crumbling shacks? Why had Daniels become serially involved with men who had so little interest in their own children, and why were they managing to get away without providing any support?

Pam Koner, an entrepreneur in Westchester, also asked these questions after reading the article. But rather than dwell on them, she decided to take action. She called a social worker in Pembroke and asked for the names of 17 families who most needed help. She rallied her friends to buy groceries for these families. They mailed the packages, and thus Family-to-Family was born. Over the past decade, Family-to-Family has identified close to two dozen needy communities, often in rural areas like Pembroke, to sponsor. Families pack up groceries for specific families, to be delivered during the last week of the month (when money tends to be tight). Families are encouraged to get to know each other, writing letters and becoming "good neighbors . . . living many miles apart," as the Family-to-Family Web site puts it.

It's an interesting idea, and Family-to-Family has had some learning experiences over the years. But broadly, Koner turned out to be on the early edge of a fascinating trend in charity: microphilanthropy.

If philanthropy is the voluntary promotion of human welfare, "microphilanthropy" means doing the same thing on a much smaller scale. Generally, it means charity that involves a direct connection between donors and projects, with donors choosing how their money is used, and nonprofits verifying cases and facilitating donations. Family-to-Family, for instance, will match your family with another family. DonorsChoose.org lets donors search through listings of classroom projects to choose ones to support. Global Giving lets the internationally minded choose from hundreds of development projects, from training midwives in Africa to promoting democracy via radio programs. The sector has seen a surge of new players, which have grown fast, and they're influencing how more established charities do their marketing. Goodwill, for instance, now has an online calculator that shows exactly how many job-search classes a donation of your old Green Day CDs can produce, in addition to sharing stories of real people Goodwill has helped.

To be sure, this emphasis on personal connections is not entirely new. When I was growing up, my family donated to the Christian Children's Fund, which sent us letters from children in Thailand who benefited from its programs. (Actually, they sent us letters from one specific child we were "sponsoring," but they were careful not to claim the money was going directly to his family—a fine line many nonprofits walk, since giving to one specific person is generally not recognized as a tax-deductible event).

Until recently, though, there has been less emphasis on this idea of connecting with neighbors in different communities or across the globe, for a few reasons. For starters, the world used to seem bigger. I remember letters from Thailand arriving on lightweight paper to keep the postage bill under control. International phone calls required a lot of money and both parties to have a phone—not exactly a given in a time before widespread cell coverage.

Even within the United States, though, part of the disconnect stemmed from what appears to be a more benevolent force: attempts to professionalize the nonprofit sector. Back in February 1979, *Forbes* magazine devoted a cover to this trend, inviting readers to learn about "America the Generous: The $9 Billion Charity Industry." Mostly highlighting the United Way, *Forbes* noted that by the mid-20th century, traditional methods of fund-raising, such as door-to-door solicitation, had become costly and ineffective. As wealthier countries developed more dignified social safety nets than the Dickensian poorhouses of yore, people in the nonprofit sector likewise wanted to move away from heart-tugging photos of abused animals or disabled children. Instead, individuals could give via payroll deductions, and United Way professionals would make decisions about where money could best be used. As United Way head William Aramony told *Forbes*, "What the United Way system provides is the rational review of how to *use* money . . . In the home-health area, the visiting nurse from the homemaker's service may not be as sexy as giving to heart or cancer, but in terms of real service—in going into the home and working with the cancer patient—that is where the action is. Giving to United Way is saying, 'I know that I don't know enough to be able to commit my money wisely.' " As *Forbes* noted, United Way's "tight controls and businesslike supervision" made it "the wave of the future in charity."

These days, the charity industry is bigger yet (Americans actually gave $35 billion to charity in 1978, but *Forbes* was counting only individual giving to health and social welfare agencies in its $9 billion figure). Individual Americans gave $227.41 billion in 2009. Foundation and institutional giving bumped that up to over $300 billion, total. Parts of the sector have become even more professionalized as multibillion-dollar foundations now employ thousands of people, some of whom have credentials from new philanthropy programs offered by universities at the undergraduate and graduate levels.

What this professionalization recognizes is that giving money away effectively, without causing more hardship, is hard work. Despite my tendency toward microphilanthropy in bus stops, I am reminded of this every time I see signs in the New York City subways imploring passengers to "Give to charity, just not here." A few years ago, I spent some time walking the streets of Seattle with Rev. Craig Rennebohm, author of *Souls in the Hands of a Tender God*, talking with his many homeless friends. The experience made it abundantly clear that homeless people often have medical or psychological issues that require professional attention. And forget whether the homeless person will "just spend the cash on booze" (as many assume)—a more pertinent problem is that a homeless person walking around with wads of cash is an easy target for violence. So, as good citizens, we are supposed to call the city directly. That way an outreach team can be dispatched to the homeless person in question.

It is all very logical. But, still, the net result of this professionalization can be a sense of alienation when it comes to giving. You give the money and let the professionals take care of it. That doesn't foster much of a sense of community for the majority of people, who aren't also going to volunteer extensively with the charities they support. As *Forbes* noted, professionalized charity via United Way payroll giving was "part of the dehumanizing process that afflicts modern life." Companies quickly told their workers exactly what the appropriate percentage was to give through United Way deductions, and as one employee told *Forbes*, "I rebel at being told how much I should contribute as a fair share. Because who got together? The same bastards who were always telling me everything else in my life—either the boss or the union—and I'm going to say 'Screw you both.'" All this, *Forbes* noted, "is giving charity the same kind of institutionalized image that is characteristic of business and government today. The human touch is missing, the personal contact; it is all machine-to-machine."

People have never been entirely comfortable with this, which is why it's no wonder that, even as charity has become more professional, people continue to give most generously to their own places of worship. God may ask you to tithe, but it helps that you're there every week, too, seeing what your money is doing.

Over the past few years, however, this impulse toward professionalized charity has started to shift. Technology tends to democratize things, and it certainly makes connecting with individuals easier. Far from waiting for the postman to arrive with thin sheets of airmail paper, I now get regular Facebook updates on what my international friends are eating for breakfast. So if you are charitably inclined, you soon start to wonder why charity should be a black box when nothing else in life is. Rather than just write a check to the Red Cross, why not choose your own clean water project to fund in Tanzania, and ask for updates along the way?

"There's a lot of evidence that this generation is used to instant access to information," says Ken Berger, president of Charity Navigator, a nonprofit watchdog. "They want more direct involvement, to be empowered in the process, and to see results more directly." Even with the rise of big charity, "real" philanthropists who can write $1 million checks have always had this ability to direct their donations and to receive feedback from the individuals helped. These days, $50 donors want to be empowered, too. They want to be treated like board members, able to know how their money is being spent and if it's producing results.

So in 2000, Bronx high school teacher Charles Best founded DonorsChoose.org, which lets teachers request funds for classroom projects online. Potential donors visiting the site can scroll through more than 20,000 projects and partially fund those they find most appealing. The most popular criterion for choosing a project is geography, with donors wanting to "support a classroom in need in their community but on the other side of the tracks," Best tells me. Then there are perennially popular keywords ("autism") or more trendy ones ("gardening projects"). Other donors hope to purchase classroom sets of books by their favorite authors. Some simply choose based on a compelling write-up. "They're looking for projects that have a whole lot of personality," Best says. "Projects where they can just feel the dedication of the teacher." In general, field trips do better than technology requests, since we all seem to hope that our money will send the next future Supreme Court justice on an inspirational trip to Washington, D.C. All donors get follow-up news, and those who give more than $100 get physical thank-you letters from the students.

It's a model that translates into international development projects as well. In 2001, two former World Bank executives launched GlobalGiving, an organization that allows donors to contribute to nonprofits running international (and domestic) projects. GlobalGiving makes a point of showing exactly what certain dollar amounts can do. A $15,000 donation will build a well in southern Sudan, but since most people won't give $15,000, this is broken down into more manageable units: $10 supplies one person permanently with clean, fresh water. In Ghana, $10 buys a bag of maize seeds; $260 purchases the inputs for farming an entire acre of maize.

This focus on small amounts having a big impact is critical to

Modest Needs (ModestNeeds.org), another pioneer in this genre. Founder Keith Taylor suffered many of the indignities of poverty when he was in graduate school, once even facing eviction after he had to choose between fixing his car and paying his rent. His boss helped him out, and he pledged to pay it forward. Now, Modest Needs, which he created in 2002, specializes in helping the working poor (who earn enough to survive but not enough to save, as Taylor puts it) pay one-time bills, so they don't wind up destitute. This is what the organization did for Susan Morrill of Maine, who tells me that "I'm one of those people that falls in that weird gap—I don't qualify for food stamps or Medicare or MaineCare." But in a winter storm, after the electricity went out, her pipes froze and backed up and burst, leaving her with holes in her floor and a nonfunctioning bathroom. She posted a request on Modest Needs, and donors helped her buy plywood and a toilet.

Microphilanthropy doesn't necessarily have to involve charity, per se. In 2005, microfinance organization Kiva began allowing people to contribute toward no-interest loans to entrepreneurs around the world. These are generally paid back (except for a few defaults, which can be written off as donations). You advance $50 to Godfrey Lwebuga of Uganda, who wishes to purchase more chickens for his poultry business, he repays the loan, and then you can use the cash to fund some other entrepreneur.

More organizations continue to come online, all with slightly different focuses. For instance, Citizen Effect, which asks individual "citizen philanthropists" to take on larger fund-raising goals by tapping their networks, launched in late 2009. Founder Dan Morrison says that "We wanted to use social media to allow people to market and promote their own projects." So Rachel, a seven-year-old girl, organizes a walk at her school to raise money for water projects; Glen rides his bike 3,000 miles; Kate and John do a chili-fest, with Citizen Effect handling the backend for these $1,000–$10,000 projects that support everything from sending Tibetan kids to summer camps to installing toilets in the Khue Dong village in Vietnam.

These organizations have experienced "phenomenal growth," says Berger; according to Charity Navigator, from 2004 to 2008 (with slightly different fiscal years), Modest Needs grew from $194,379 to $2.7 million in revenue, GlobalGiving grew from $508,653 to $7.4 million, and DonorsChoose.org grew from $2.8 million to $18 million.

"Clearly they are here to stay and are part of the landscape of how people are served by nonprofits," Berger says. While these nonprofits retain the right to direct funds more broadly (part of the tricky issue on IRS regulations about direct giving), they usually do follow donors' wishes and always offer follow-up—often in the form of thank-you notes or e-mails—which extends the happiness from a donation and gives you a boost every time you check in.

WHAT IS FAIR?

The rise of microphilanthropy does raise real issues, however, when it comes to who benefits. I sought out donors/lenders to these organizations to ask about how they made their choices. Some had pretty straightforward criteria. They supported only projects helping women, for instance, in countries where women do not have many rights. Others had more quirky requirements. California mom Amy Markoff Johnson has an autistic son with dietary issues, and when we talked he was eating a lot of yams. "I cook like ten yams a day," she said. So when she found a listing on Kiva for a small business owner who sold yams, she was quick to chip in. "I feel close to them," she says.

But she has felt a little strange about this because "I don't trust my own judgment, that my money is going to the absolute best place.

I'm funding a person who's selling sweet potatoes because my kid eats them. It's something that strikes my fancy." Is that a solid reason for giving someone your money?

It's a good question. Microphilanthropy is prone to donor whim and to donor assumptions about who is worthy and who is not. I spoke recently with Marilyn Assenheim, a New Jersey resident who'd requested money on Modest Needs for a tub-to-shower conversion. Not all Modest Needs requests are filled. Hers was filled quickly, in part because it was compelling, but also because she sent around the request to her own e-mail list. Her friends forwarded it and (she suspects) chipped in their own money. In other words, her need was met because she was better connected, and Modest Needs facilitated what could be thought of as a community barn raising.

The issue with microphilanthropy is it favors the charismatic, the attractive, and the most articulate among those in need. It conjures up all the old problems that professional charity was trying to avoid— that parents would send their children to beg in the streets because they were more effective at inspiring empathy than adults. This isn't just the case for human-centered donations, either. Recently, I wrote a piece for *City Journal* on the public-private partnerships that support many of New York City's parks. These partnerships have done amazing things to turn around a number of the city's properties. But it should come as no surprise that such parks as Central Park (surrounded by some of the country's richest zip codes), or the High Line in Chelsea (ditto), have an easier time raising money than a playground in a lower-middle-class section of Queens. In theory, private fund-raising for charismatic parks should enable the city government to concentrate its funds on lesser-known parks, but one can also envision a scenario in which voters, knowing that their favorite parks are privately funded, no longer support generous public funding for other parks, which then fall into disrepair. This is not inevitable. In New York, Bette Midler has made a point of funding parks in not-so-nice neighborhoods. Smart nonprofits can also nudge donors toward choosing projects that the organization has deemed most worthy. Charles Best's team at DonorsChoose.org, for instance, has come up with an algorithm for choosing the four classrooms that appear on the first page of projects when you visit the site. "Those four are not randomized," he says. They tend to be in high-poverty districts, have received partial funding (meaning other donors have already donated to them), and are close enough to the finish line that an individual donor might be able to put them over the top. Still, the fairness issue is real.

Donor-directed giving also raises issues of efficiency. Technology has made bundling many small donations cheap, but when microphilanthropy moves beyond cash, the issue gets thornier—which brings us back to Family-to-Family. After Pam Koner started shipping her boxes of groceries to Pembroke, she became a media darling, which makes sense given her wonderful story. How many thousands of us read that Pembroke article in the *New York Times* and did nothing except cluck? As producers from CBS's *The Early Show* and elsewhere filmed Koner and her boxes, more people wanted to get involved. So Koner pondered how to scale up.

First, she had her families mail packages to specific families, just as she had always done. The pledge to donors was that each donor would be the last person to touch the groceries before the recipient family opened the box.

But the more Koner thought about grinding poverty in places like Pembroke, the more flaws she saw in this methodology. Families buying groceries for Family-to-Family were generally paying retail for individual items at supermarkets. Wouldn't it be more efficient to buy in bulk for the 450 families they soon found themselves serving? A dollar could go a lot further that way. So Family-to-Family began encouraging people to give cash.

Then Koner proceeded to ask other questions. Why, for instance, are people starving at the end of the month in the United States? Maybe, rather than focusing on giving groceries, Family-to-Family could start looking at the root causes of poverty. As the saying goes, give a man a fish and you feed him for a day; teach him to fish and you feed him for a lifetime. There were many possible programs suggested by this line of thought. Maybe they could help people find jobs or train them for jobs they might get later. Or maybe they could focus on family counseling and encouraging fathers to support their children. Or they could go down the route of advocacy, and lobby for more generous food stamp benefits or a different way of distributing them, so people wouldn't experience such stark times at the end of the month, as LaCheir Daniels's family memorably demonstrated.

All these are important issues and could help address hunger more broadly. Except that as Koner thought this through, she had a realization. The point of the original *New York Times* article was that, after 40 years of a War on Poverty, involving billions more dollars than Family-to-Family was ever going to raise, the federal government still hadn't solved problems like those in Pembroke. The place was a graveyard of people's good intentions. That isn't to say that more couldn't be done. Koner maintains that we could end hunger "if it was a value of our culture." Fundamentally, though, as Fountain's article put it, the problem is as much "hopelessness" as anything else, and any solution to that is a long way down the line.

But here's something Koner could do: "I can make sure there is food on the table the last week of the month," she says, at least for a few families. She could help people in limited circumstances establish connections with other families living a different life, and at least let the children in these recipient families know that another life exists. And she could sustain this by giving donor families a way to feel that their gifts were doing genuine good, directly.

And so, Family-to-Family has been "returning to our original model," Koner says. "We're going back to the box." It may not be the most efficient way of addressing hunger, but the opportunity to shop for an individual family is what makes Family-to-Family unique, is what makes giving meaningful for donors, and is what makes them likely to keep at it. When people keep at something over time, they do more good than if they decide to stop, and they'll be more likely to keep up the good work if they feel engaged and convinced that what they're doing is paying off. Indeed, I suspect the nonprofit sector's trend toward more personalization and accountability is a big reason individual giving didn't really fall in 2009, even as the stock market and housing values tanked and the unemployment rate nearly doubled. When people know more they give more. Even when times are tight. When people's giving to charity is based on their own happiness, charitable giving can compete more effectively with other priorities, rather than being chucked along with so much excess consumer spending. In the long run, this makes people do more good than if they gave for completely altruistic reasons.

HOW TO GIVE

So that's the argument for considering happiness when making charitable decisions. But how do we put that into practice? How can we give in a way that lets our limited dollars create joy in our own lives, while still doing as much good as possible? After hunting through research on money and happiness, I've come up with a four-step process.

1. **Figure out how much you can give . . . sort of.** Many personal finance books suggest creating a budget for giving just as you'd allocate money to housing, transportation, food, and so on. This is fine, as long as you remember that whatever you set aside is an inherently slippery number. Household income is more variable than peo-

ple assume, as are household expenditures. If you're willing to sleep on friends' couches, you might be able to give 75 percent of your income away. Or perhaps you're officially giving zero, but your entire livelihood is one of service—e.g. working long hours for low pay in an inner-city school or providing medical care to refugees. Only you can determine if the good you're doing for humanity is more important than the cash (and perhaps this is what Al Gore was thinking when he and Tipper famously gave $353 to charity in 1997—although I doubt his political opponents shared this view).

The average person gives roughly 3 percent of her income. A tithe, 10 percent, is also a popular number, one with religious weight to it. Greg Rohlinger, pastor of the Palm Valley Community Church in Goodyear, Arizona, speculates that God created the tithe for a reason. "I think 10 percent is enough that it hurts every paycheck, but doesn't make me unable to live in the community," he says. After all, "God could have said 90 percent. He can have whatever he wants. We can be thankful he said ten." As for whether this is 10 percent before or after taxes, Rohlinger says "that's between you and the Lord." He personally wants "the Lord to be first in front of the IRS, but I don't get into it with my church." Instead he asks "whether you want to be blessed off the gross or the net."

This idea of framing giving in terms of the blessing one receives from it sounds a little strange, but as the studies cited at the beginning of this chapter found, pro-social spending (which includes charity) is one of the few things that clearly buy happiness. Rohlinger truly believes this. Indeed, Palm Valley Community Church has a 90-day money-back guarantee on tithing. If you tithe for 90 days, and decide that God hasn't blessed your life by more than you're giving, you'll get your money back. No questions asked, and no public shaming is involved. "We do not put your name in the bulletin," Rohlinger says, if you ask for a refund. He has stories of new tithers who've received tax refund checks out of the blue, compensation for work done years ago that they'd long since written off, or promotions they didn't even know they were in line for. Nonetheless, "I don't think it's biblical to say Publishers Clearing House is going to show up at your door with a $10 million check because you tithed for 90 days," he says. The blessings are often in the form of feeling more tied to your church and its members, who will then help you through a tough patch. This is what he suggested when I mentioned a firestorm over tithing that erupted at DailyWorth, a financial Web site for women. A reader signed up for a financial makeover with expert Liz Pulliam Weston. The reader had taken on some debt to pay for an international adoption, yet continued to tithe. Weston suggested she stop tithing for a bit, which the reader decided not to do. I asked if this was wise. Surely God values adoption as giving, too, right? Rohlinger suggested I was framing the issue the wrong way. This was a situation where "the church has to be the church. In our small groups, when there is a financial need, we encourage people to meet it." In other words, an expensive adoption doesn't mean you stop tithing. It means you ask your fellow church members to tap their networks to help you pay for the adoption.

Our family doesn't give 10 percent, though I find the idea appealing. You can pick a number or percentage if you want, but keep in mind that if you get into a cause, money may start to drift into the charitable category from other areas, because you'll consider sending five Indian girls to school more fun than a round of golf. This is why I think that an even more important early step than budgeting is to:

2. **Discover what really motivates you.** When you skim a newspaper, what kinds of articles draw you in? What communities have you visited or lived in that you'd like to improve? What do you credit as a turning point in your life? (Yes, yes, this is why everyone wants to fund field trips on DonorsChoose.org, but there's something to it.) What issue *really* ticks you off?

These questions involve serious thought. They are part of the larger process of getting to know oneself but are no less important than other decisions people belabor, such as what movie to watch tonight. You can simply look at the brochures that nonprofits send you in the mail. Or you can take a more holistic approach, which is what Jennifer Page is doing.

Page, a former television producer, turned 40 not long ago and found herself pondering various Big Questions. "This might sound trite, but have you seen the musical *Avenue Q?*" she wrote me. "The guy in it is looking to find his purpose in life at the start of the musical. I'm looking to find mine." Broadly, she hit upon the idea of using her time and money to make life significantly better for 100 people, a project she started dubbing Help 100. "I don't think I'm capable of changing the world," she said. But 100 people seemed doable. Sort of. Because, really, how do you best go about doing that? She started with three approaches:

A. "Trying out easy ideas that anyone can do . . . things that don't need loads of money or too much time—not everyone can quit their job and volunteer in Africa for five years, because of children, elderly relatives, relationships, career commitments. . . ."

B. "Keeping a blog that perhaps will develop into a book and Web site in order to give other people ideas of what they could do. . . ."

C. "Trying to find a big project that I can really focus on. I think that I will probably help 90 percent of my people that way. But I don't know what that is yet. Right now, the focus for me is on being open: being open to suggestions, to hearing stories, to putting myself in the way of things—I mean, going to events where I might stumble upon someone that needs help with their project or a small charity that could do with some momentum."

She made lists of different interests: education, microfinance, Africa. She made lists of her skills: teaching, film making, writing, organizing things. She got intriguing leads as she tried different projects. She spent a day volunteering at a homeless center and one morning a week working with a local mental health charity. She ran a weekend course on loneliness. She became a "befriender" for a local charity that works with lonely elderly people. She joined a committee that was fund-raising to build a well in Africa.

She wasn't sure quite how this would all turn out, but she was "discovering what suits my mode of working and my lifestyle and what doesn't." Coming up with a highly motivating charitable vision is a bit like finding the right idea for starting a business, or locating an enterprise you'd like to become a major investor in. It takes time and searching to see a problem and a doable solution. Once you find this motivating vision, though, you can derive great joy from focusing your time and cash.

3. **Do the bulk of your giving through one organization, in a way that builds community.** If giving is about recognizing that we are social creatures, then it's smart to give in a way that nurtures social ties. This is the brilliance of tithing—the bulk of your giving goes to your local church, where it supports the programs that create a community that will support you. But this is far from the only way to give.

Consider an organization like Impact Austin. Rebecca Powers, a former sales rep for IBM, started Impact Austin in 2003 after reading a story in *People* magazine about a Cincinnati woman who had consolidated $1,000 gifts from numerous women to create larger gifts. Powers, who was going through a difficult time personally, decided to replicate this in Austin. She started with a handful of members and now is up to 542 women, each giving $1,000, which they turn into five $108,400 grants (she raises administrative costs separately). Impact Austin vets area nonprofits and then chooses two finalists in each of five categories, such as education and health. Members vote on which finalists to fund in each category at a big June event. Member Lorie Marrero describes it. "We use paper ballots and they are counted right then, and we get to know the winners very shortly afterward. This is incredibly exciting—it should be a reality show. People are crying from happiness, from being touched by the results." The six-figure grants, sometimes given to organizations with budgets as low as $400,000, have funded everything from sterilizing feral cats to working with Goodwill to create green jobs.

As for community, Austin has a lot of transplants from elsewhere. Impact Austin gives women who are new to town a quick way to plug into a circle of women who can write $1,000 checks—not a bad place to network if you're starting a business or are interested in learning about new job opportunities. People meet clients and vendors without the fake atmosphere of many cocktail parties. "Women love to give this way," says Powers. "We love to collaborate and create change and celebrate our results." Some members just write checks, but others get involved in the vetting committees, which offer another way to deepen social ties.

The $1,000 price of admission is larger than many people might give to charity in one shot, but a stretch number like this can also be clarifying. "For me, this simplifies my giving to one annual check," says Marrero. "No more decisions to make about $25 for this, $50 for that—I say no to all of those now and just give this one $1,000 amount." This is generally a more efficient way to give because of the costs to a nonprofit associated with keeping lots of small donors informed. The postage for a newsletter is the same if you give $60 or $600; better if 10 people each gave $600 to one favorite group than each of them giving $60 to 10. Marrero also reports that there are psychological benefits to concentrating her giving. It has "changed my opinion of what philanthropy means," she says. "I used to think that philanthropists were just people like Bill Gates, but now I self-identify with that term, and that changes my outlook on lots of things in my community." She has the power to make a difference.

The one caveat to this is that, as we saw in the research that opened this chapter, the size of people's gifts had no effect on happiness. Given that each individual donation can give a happiness boost, you might enjoy giving most if your $3,000 pledge to an organization is paid out in the form of twelve $250 donations, with an e-mail alert sent to you every time the money is deducted from your checking account, rather than in one fell swoop. That way, you get to enjoy the happiness boost multiple times. I also think there's a place for a few small if not entirely efficient donations, which is why I think you should . . .

4. **Give yourself some philanthropy fun money.** Concentrate the bulk of your giving on a few organizations, but leave about 20 percent of your total charitable budget unrestricted, so you can dole it out to things that strike your fancy. In the context of buying happiness, I can think of little more fun than going through life with the mind-set of always looking for ways to make the world better for $5–$20. And not just via nonprofits. Spending money on other people qualifies as pro-social spending whether there's a tax deduction involved or not. Here are some quick ways to practice random acts of microphilanthropy:

▶ On occasion, leave a ridiculously large tip.

▶ On a regular basis, leave a good one.

▶ Donate new crayons to a kindergarten or Sunday school class.

▸ Pay for a babysitter for a young couple in your church, or offer to babysit for them.

▸ Give great gifts—thinking of how you might delight another person is a great way to feel some delight yourself.

▸ Pay the bus fare for someone whose pass expired.

▸ Take the office intern out to lunch.

▸ Leave a gift card on someone's doorstep.

▸ Donate $20 to the first charity request you see in your Facebook feed.

▸ Buy an umbrella for someone caught in the rain (as a Pittsburgh group called Here You Go has done).

▸ Pay the toll of the person behind you on the highway.

As you spend your charity fun money, keep a list of how you're doing so. Then read it over whenever you can. Your workday may have been a total disaster. Your teenagers may hate you, and you haven't made it to the gym in weeks. But it's hard not to feel rich and happy when staring at two dozen ways the world is better because you're in it.

CHAPTER 9

Another Way to Invest

Michigan in February can be a bleak place, but my 26-year-old breakfast companion, Margarita Barry, was far more ebullient than the weather. One thing this serial entrepreneur wanted to discuss as we sat in a cozy Plymouth coffee shop, looking out at the snow: her hoped-for launch of Detroit-based 71 POP, a retail space where a rotating group of creative types could sell their wares on a trial basis before opening their own stores. "They can get their feet wet without dealing with any of the hard stuff," she said. "I run it for them. They're earning money and getting foot traffic." If a product line turned out to be a hit, the designer would have a good track record for signing a lease elsewhere. "I have tenants lined up already," she told me. The building (a rehabbed space at 71 Garfield in Detroit's Sugar Hill Arts District) was ready to go. Everyone she talked to thought it was a great idea.

Now, there was just the matter of getting start-up funding.

I was mostly there to interview Margarita about her existing business (a Web site called I Am Young Detroit), so I didn't think too much about 71 POP until a few months later, when I found an annual financial chore on my to-do list: making a contribution to my 401(k). I hope I never have to retire, but if the U.S. government wants to give me a tax deduction for stashing money away, something I'd do without the deduction, I will make my contribution to a balanced portfolio of domestic and international exchange traded funds. Since I don't have a regular monthly income (I get paid by the project) I tend to make this annual contribution in one big check when I'm feeling flush. Then I spend some time over the next few months executing orders for VT (The Vanguard Total World Stock Index Fund), IVV (iShares S&P 500 Index Fund), and other such investments.

Around this same time, I got a message from Margarita that she was trying to raise $8,000 for 71 POP via Kickstarter, a Web site that bundles small contributions to help launch creative projects. Clicking over to the site, I was drawn in by Margarita's promise to create "an ever-transforming collage of creativity and a unique way to shop local" in Detroit. So I sent her $25, becoming one of 101 initial 71 POP supporters.

Guess which investment was more fun?

If you think like most other rational people, my ETFs should be. According to the usual retirement literature, over the next 30 years, my $5,000 contribution will grow to roughly $50,000—an amount that can enable all sorts of enjoyable golden years activities. Backing 71 POP, in theory, offers no financial returns for me whatsoever.

If you take a closer look, however, the situation is more complicated than that. In my professional life, I write about entrepreneurship and the creative economy all the time. One of my biggest hassles is coming up with real people to write about, beyond the usual suspects whose press releases keep showing up in my inbox, and hence showing up in everyone else's inboxes, too. One of the rewards Margarita offered her supporters is a "print 'zine" with write-ups on the folks tromping through 71 POP. Can I turn those leads into more than $250 worth of stories, the equivalent return over the next 30 years that I'd get in my 401(k)? I would say the odds are good.

But it's not just the money that makes my 71 POP contribution more exciting than my other investments. Broadly, investing in the stock market enables a system that gives big companies the ability to grow and create more jobs and . . . la la la. Let's face it. Unless you're the kind of person who dreams of having a Bloomberg terminal in your living room, there is nothing inherently fun about purchasing an incredibly tiny share of the Russell 2000. We should do it, for the same reasons we should eat kale. It is a sober adult thing to do, with long-term payoffs, even if the immediate effect is less clear. Investing in small entrepreneurial projects, on the other hand, lets us use our money in ways where we can see the results while building personal connections. I like knowing that my money is being used to create opportunities for other people who, like the emerging designers and artists of 71 POP, are often going to school or working full-time in addition to their creative endeavors. Not only could these people use a little support, I could, if I wanted, meet and get to know them— something I'm not sure I could say about the CEOs of most S&P 500–listed firms.

So in the context of buying happiness, I think we should expand the definition of investment. Broadly, investing means to commit resources to an endeavor with the hope of achieving a return. This can mean buying stocks or other standard investment products—as it should for much of your investment budget—but it could also mean creating opportunities for other people as you buy time to focus on your highest-value work. It can mean using your money to get start-ups off the ground (possible in limited ways even if you don't meet certain net worth requirements from the Securities and Exchange Commission—and increasingly efficient if you do). It can even mean spending with the goal of creating a thriving local economy that makes your community an attractive place to live. There may not be a direct path between buying a latte at an independent coffee shop and having your compensation rise because people are flocking into town and creating a huge demand for your employer's services, but if you think about it, there was no direct connection between owning Lehman Brothers stock and prosperity either. In the first scenario, at least you'll get a latte and the social capital of a neighborhood coffee shop where people know you out of the deal.

The empowering truth in these stretched times is that all of us have the ability to encourage the growth of jobs and the hope and happiness that can come from them. We have a choice in how to spend our money, and we can put resources toward people rather than things, and in particular, toward people in our own communities or other communities we care about. Done right, investing is the ultimate in pro-social spending. You create opportunities for other people who then create opportunities for you. It's a nice complement to traditional ideas of net worth—and a lot more entertaining than executing another order for IVV.

THE HAPPY INVESTOR

Over the past few years, as the U.S. unemployment rate rose toward double digits before inching back down, job creation has become a national obsession. Less talked about is how, exactly, jobs get created. In general, a job has its genesis when a business owner decides that the cost to employ someone is less than the additional revenue that employee will create. These metrics become less straightforward as the firm gets bigger (does anyone know how much revenue any given midlevel manager is responsible for?), but the clarity of a new firm may be a key part of the equation; according to statistics from the Kauffman Foundation (which focuses on entrepreneurship), all the net job growth in the U.S. economy over the past few decades has come from firms that are less than five years old. With established companies, as a group, every time a job is created in one place, another one disappears in another. Not so with rapidly scaling start-ups, which can go from 0 to 60 employees (or 600 or 6,000) in a matter of months.

Because of this reality, entrepreneurs are job creators, which is a heady thought if you've gone down that career path. Business owners tell me that hiring those first employees is a terrifying but magical moment. It is terrifying because—much like becoming a new parent—suddenly you aren't responsible for just yourself. You have to meet a payroll no matter what. In the deepest days of the recession in late 2009, according to one American Express poll, 27 percent of small business owners had stopped taking a salary, and 17 percent were working a second job to make ends meet. That's on top of running their businesses! Clearly, this can create a lot of stress. On the other hand, it feels "absolutely amazing" to make a hire, says Jessica Brondo, who owns The Edge, an educational consulting company. After doing most of the back-office work herself for years, she finally hired an office manager who's doing "such a great job. It's really been a great lesson. When you give someone the tools and train them properly on what works for you, they can do just as good a job as you," she says. Plus, "[it's] giving me the time to focus on other things"—namely, growing the business, so she can hire more people. Seeing your employees buy homes and go on vacations and knowing that your business idea enabled them to do so is a feeling of accomplishment that is hard to match in anything else we do.

Most of us aren't in the position to hire people full-time, of course. Nonetheless, we can still use our resources to get in on some of the fun of creating opportunities for people.

One way to do that, if you are not an entrepreneur, is to steer money toward entrepreneurs who are creating jobs.

The rules on this are—as with so much in the financial world—

complicated. In order to offer shares to the public, a company in the United States has to fulfill various requirements from the Securities and Exchange Commission (SEC). Generally, a company doesn't have an initial public offering (IPO) until it is quite large and, dot-com bubble notwithstanding, past the start-up phase. The SEC and individual states have their own rules on who can invest in nonpublic companies. These rules are designed to protect people with limited assets from losing their money in unscrupulous ventures. If you're worth millions—an "accredited" investor basically needs a net worth north of $1 million, excluding a primary residence, or else meets certain income requirements—the SEC figures you are a big boy or girl and can decide for yourself what is snake oil and what is not.

What's fascinating to me about all this is how few people who *do* have a net worth of more than $1 million invest in early-stage companies through so-called angel investor funds, or even on a personal basis. More than 5 million U.S. households have over $1 million in investible assets, and nowhere near that number invest this way. The discrepancy seems to arise from cultural attitudes, with people who've cashed out of other start-ups feeling more comfortable with the process than people who've made their money in conventional jobs.

The problem with this scenario is that—because early-stage investing is risky—angel investors tend to invest in ideas dreamed up by people they identify with. Wealth patterns being what they are, this means that companies founded by white men have an easier time tapping into equity funding than companies founded by other folks. Women own close to one third of all U.S. businesses. But women-owned businesses receive well under 10 percent of equity financing. The hope is that more diverse angels will seek out and fund more diverse companies. So if you are a woman or person of color with a high net worth, there is a real societal need for your cash to be put to work. "There are a lot more people who could be doing it," says Patricia Greene, a professor of entrepreneurship at Babson College in Wellesley, Massachusetts. Investing in start-ups "is risky, but frankly, right now, what else is there to invest in?" (One thing mitigating some of that risk: technology is adding liquidity to the market for alternative investments. SecondMarket.com, for instance, lets accredited investors buy shares in some nonpublic companies in a very straightforward fashion).

Of course, there have to be exceptions to the minimum net worth rules, or America's entrepreneurial culture wouldn't work. Your average Joe starting a restaurant doesn't know enough millionaires to get start-up funds only from them. So (generally) you can have a certain number of regular investors in your private company so long as you have a substantial relationship with these people. Joe can get $15,000 from his sister-in-law to start a business without this being a legal no-no.

I imagine most people haven't thought much about these areas of securities law. The reason they are entering the public consciousness now is that "crowdfunding" is a rapidly growing component of Web 2.0 (or whichever edition we're on at the moment). Crowdfunding means pooling resources from a network of people for a project. Think fans—rather than a record label—sponsoring a rock band's tour in exchange for tickets and T-shirts. Or readers—rather than a publisher—paying an author to commission a new book in exchange for autographed copies and listings in the acknowledgments.

It's a new field but growing rapidly. Kickstarter, launched in 2009, allows any creative type to post a project online and ask friends, family, and strangers for token funds (usually $25–$100 apiece) in exchange for rewards. Two years later, it has raised $40 million for roughly 7,500 projects. Other Web sites such as RocketHub, Indie-GoGo, and PeerBackers have also enabled thousands of people to raise modest sums (roughly $2,000–$10,000 per project) for everything from documentaries to books to an artisanal baker pledging birthday cakes for life to anyone giving $500 or more to defray her business start-up costs.

Due to SEC rules, at most of these sites, backers must be offered rewards rather than anything monetary. So the reasons for contributing are mixed: to help a friend, or because people are "starting to see it as a discovery tool, a way to find people and find talent on the cusp that is emerging," says Vladimir Vukicevic, cofounder of RocketHub. Plus, backers are drawn by "the ability to make an impact"— that $25 can help create something that otherwise wouldn't exist. And sometimes, the rewards are cool in their own right. In 2010, Regan Wann, proprietor of Through the Looking Glass Fine Teas & Gifts in Shelbyville, Kentucky, asked backers on RocketHub for help moving into a larger space. "People came out of the woodwork and I learned that what I'm doing mattered to a lot of people beyond just me," she reports. She gave people tea samplers and—one day as an incentive—agreed to name a tea blend after a randomly chosen supporter (a reward she also offered to anyone giving at the $500 level). So now Through the Looking Glass sells "Razi's Blend," a concoction of orange, green, and black teas that the lady who won the drawing blended herself. No matter how much you spend at Starbucks, you won't get your own tea blend. If you live in Shelbyville, on the other hand, not only will a small investment help create a thriving independent tea shop where you can meet clients, conduct interviews, and so forth, you could help create a place where everyone knows your name. Literally. Because it's on the menu.

As the plethora of crowdfunding sites aim for different niches, some, such as Peerbackers, have started to focus exclusively on entrepreneurs, though even these usually require that entrepreneurs dole out rewards, not money. "It's the NPR model," explains Peerbackers cofounder Sally Outlaw, with fans supporting something they like in exchange for a tote bag. They decided it was important "not to bump up against SEC requirements."

It's not impossible for investors to get financial returns, though. ProFounder, a new site launched in late 2010, creates an easier process for entrepreneurs to send invites and company financial specs to people in the friends-and-family category who are legally allowed to invest. In exchange for fronting capital, the investors get a percentage of revenue for a certain number of years. "If you're creating a for-profit business, we thought that's a logical and fair way to reward something," says cofounder Dana Mauriello. So, for instance, BucketFeet, a company that makes "wearable art" sneakers, raised $60,000 from 33 investors by promising 5 percent of revenue for three years. ProFounder's most innovative contribution, though, may be its Group Advisors program. In cities including Albuquerque, Honolulu, and Atlanta, ProFounder's group advisors facilitate social events, programming, and community-building activities that can bring together people who might invest money locally with those who need it for their companies. The SEC does not define how many times you need to have a beer with someone before you have a relationship, but over time, someone can become a friend. This new friend can invest reasonable amounts of money in local entrepreneurs' ideas and then frequent these same businesses as they grow.

Another option for making money by investing in entrepreneurs is through peer-to-peer lending sites including Prosper and LendingClub. These sites let users bid (via interest rates) on small loans to individuals. Many of these individual loans are for debt consolidation, but in June 2011, the *Wall Street Journal* reported a sharp uptick, over the previous year, in loans whose purpose was to fund a business. A recent visit to Prosper turned up opportunities to kick in toward a $14,000 loan to a business wishing to purchase computers, $5,000 to a beauty salon owner wishing to buy equipment, and $15,000 to a vending machine company whose owner wanted to add more machines to his routes. Some business owners who seek out Prosper or LendingClub don't have good enough credit to qualify for traditional small business loans, but others just want to borrow smaller amounts than a commercial bank would be interested in providing. And even some good credit risks have gotten caught in the recent credit crunch. Default rates can be high on these sites, but it can be fun to stash a small bit of money there and see what you get back (Prosper and LendingClub claim average returns in the 9–10 percent range for investors).

THE $1,750 QUESTION

Even if you're not looking to invest in start-ups, there are other options for investing in people, in the hopes of getting a return. One solution is to pay someone to do a project that will make life easier—and perhaps more profitable—for you. In short, outsource. Sometimes people feel funny about outsourcing certain tasks (particularly on the domestic front), but the alternate way of viewing such arrangements is that you are giving people jobs and opportunities that they wouldn't have if you did everything yourself. Where's the downside in that?

I was reminded of this in October 2010 while reading a tongue-in-cheek column Joel Stein wrote in *Time*. This was in the middle of the congressional debate over whether or not to abolish the Bush-era tax cuts for people earning over $250,000 a year. Stein mentioned that, if the cuts remained, he would get to keep an extra $1,753. He posed the question of how he might spend this money in the most patriotic way possible.

Economist Mark Zandi gave him a serious answer. If Stein wanted to do the most good in the short term, he said, he should create a chunk of a job. "Have a good temp assistant come in once or twice a week and do your expenses," he said, so Stein could focus on writing his columns.

Stein wound up not doing this (he figured out he didn't actually have a taxable income over $250,000 after he deducted his business

expenses and local taxes), but I think it's an interesting thought experiment. To whom could you pay $1,750 for doing some task that it
doesn't make sense for you to spend your time doing? With the
growth of the moonlighting culture in America, you could probably
buy 100 hours of someone's time for $17.50 an hour. Hiring someone
as an on-site employee involves dealing with various regulations and
taxes, but someone who did projects on her own time, with you dic-
tating the outcome but not the means, wouldn't be subject to the
same rules. Payments to a small incorporated business also don't in-
cur the same reporting and withholding requirements.

So what would you do with 100 extra man-hours? What might
that enable in your life? You might hire someone to:

▸ Create the scrapbooks or photo books about your kids and
vacations that you will never get around to doing

▸ Declutter your garage, set up a yard sale, or sell the items
on eBay

▸ Create a promotional Web site for you

▸ Get bids from contractors on some nagging home projects
and supervise their completion

▸ Paint stunning murals on your kids' bedroom walls

▸ Guide you on a weeklong trip down the Mississippi

▸ Go through all your receipts and organize such an efficient
financial system that you will never miss a deduction again

▸ Take care of your lawn and garden for the entire summer

▸ Do all your birthday, anniversary, and holiday shopping
for you and make sure stamped, addressed greeting cards
show up on your desk five days before all pertinent occasions

▶ Manage your social media presence and research/write blog posts

▶ Teach you a foreign language so you can take that promotion that comes with an overseas transfer

Are there any projects you'd love to attempt but have told yourself "there just aren't enough hours in the day"? There are a few places to find a virtual assistant (such as Craigslist and HireMyMom. com). Work your network and post a job description on Facebook; someone probably knows someone who'd be perfect. Outsourcing takes advantage of the same economic principle that leads nations to trade with one another and companies to contract with outside accountants and legal firms. Even if you might be able to design a reasonably attractive blog, somebody else probably does it better and faster. This frees up time for you to focus on what you do best, and hopefully make more money while you're at it. That way you'll achieve every bit as much of a return as you would with other investments—while giving opportunities to someone else as well.

Finally, a well-rounded alternative investment portfolio might require that you . . .

CHANGE HOW YOU SHOP

Even the way we purchase things can have an effect on our communities, with subtle shifts increasing the likelihood that our resources will generate a return in social capital.

Over the past few decades, urban renewal has become as trendy as crowdfunding, with cities laboring to understand what sparks commerce within their limits. It's a difficult question. Getting a large corporation to place its headquarters or a factory in your town is a big win, but it can be as hard to guarantee as winning the lottery. So what about other options?

To answer this question, in 2004, research firm Civic Economics undertook a study of Andersonville, a district on Chicago's north side with lots of small independent stores arranged in a way that encouraged foot traffic. The district was pondering the pros and cons of bringing in chain stores, and so the researchers combed through the books of several local independent merchants and compared them with financial statements filed by publicly traded chains. The study claimed that, for every $100 spent at an independent store, $68 remained in the community, in the form of direct local spending: local wages and benefits, the local owner's profits, payments to local suppliers and local charitable contributions. With chain stores, that number fell to $43 (since the profits largely went to shareholders based elsewhere, and charitable giving followed corporate rather than local priorities). Chain stores overall produced more revenue, so if a town's only concern was sales tax revenue, that would seem to point in one direction, though the study claimed this was because chain stores were bigger. Revenue per square foot was comparable (actually, the independents pulled in a few more dollars per square foot).

The number that struck me as most intriguing, though—and the hardest to spin—was the percentage of revenue spent on wages. Independent merchants spent 28 percent of their revenue on wages, and chains spent 23 percent. Civic Economics confirmed the direction of this difference in a 2008 study of Grand Rapids, Michigan. The firm compared independent and chain merchants in multiple categories. For every $1 million in revenue at grocery stores, chains employed 4.2 people and local merchants employed 5.0. For every $1 million in revenue at pharmacies, chains employed 1.9 people and local pharmacies employed 3.3. At restaurants, $1 million in revenue corresponded to 14.8 jobs at local establishments and 9.7 jobs for chains. With banks, locally owned, independent firms spent 1.8 percent of assets on labor, whereas chains spent 1.1 percent. For any given revenue amount, local businesses had higher payroll requirements than chains. In other words, local businesses spent more on people.

This makes a lot of sense. Independent merchants would have trouble achieving the same economies of scale as a chain. They are often doing their own marketing and procurement and don't have corporate policies that dictate store layouts or even bagging procedures that require the least amount of labor. This is not necessarily good or bad. It's just optimizing different things. Publicly traded chains may be trying to maximize shareholder value by keeping costs low, while smart independent merchants could use their higher manpower requirements to carve out distinctive niches that would keep them from needing to compete directly on price.

This is what Nikki Furrer has done with Pudd'nhead Books in St. Louis. She started the company on a shoestring in October 2008 and continues to "live below the poverty line," she reports, as "everything goes right back into the business." She focuses on a high-service model, even though with books, price competition isn't as much an issue since many prices are written directly on the dust jackets. Her staff has read enough of the books in the store to do on-target recommendations. So on target, in fact, that Furrer's Web site warns customers that if they're buying a gift for someone and describe the person the same way year to year, the staff may recommend the same book. The knowledgeable staff members create such a pleasant atmosphere—particularly in a well-curated children's section—that Pudd'nhead Books is now expanding and moving into a bigger space. It broke even its first year, saw revenue rise 20 percent the next year, and in January 2011 had receipts up 50 percent from the comparable period the year before. Furrer achieved all this even as Borders filed for bankruptcy.

This manpower difference suggests a simple mantra for mindful consumers: want to create jobs? Buy local. That is, switch some of your shopping to independent, locally owned stores. The Civic Economics study of Grand Rapids claimed that a 10 percent shift in market share to locally owned firms could create 1,614 jobs in Kent County. This might be optimistic. If local firms got bigger, they might achieve some of the economies of scale that eluded them before. But it probably wouldn't zero out, and what makes shopping fun is when you can turn it into more of an experience rather than a sheer acquisition of goods. Finding something distinctive in a pleasantly different shopping environment will do that. That doesn't mean you have to waste time and money trying to switch all your shopping in categories where it doesn't make sense. If you need Pampers, you can buy those at Diapers.com. If you desperately need a frozen pizza at 9 P.M. on a Tuesday, stop by Wal-Mart. If you need a $50 gift, however, and don't care what it is, that might be a good opportunity to browse the stacks at Pudd'nhead, or visit 71 POP, rather than a chain.

But, you may wonder, how does this count as investing? Buying local may create jobs, but what's in it for me?

The answer has to do with a broad definition of wealth. One of the best predictors of human happiness is having strong, positive social ties. Some of this comes from our immediate families—one reason to have that extra kid we talked about in chapter 6—but many of us have to make our own extended families. We do this when we help create thriving local communities where people know each others' names and get to know one another better over time. You can try to find such a community by hunting through magazines with cover stories on "best places to live." You can hope one comes into being. Or you can actively use your money to try to create one.

One of the best examples I've seen of this, like Margarita Barry's 71 POP, is in Detroit. My first stop on the trip when I interviewed her was to Slows Bar BQ, where I was supposed to meet a handful of area entrepreneurs. One of these turned out to be the co-owner of Slows himself, Phil Cooley. He's a fascinating character: a former runway model from a well-to-do family who decided to open a high-end barbecue joint across from the vacant ruins of Michigan Central Station. His initial investment was lots of sweat equity and an advance on his inheritance. The pulled pork on his menu is certainly good, but Detroit—at a civic low point lately that culminated with the auto bailouts—was not used to destination restaurants. Slows filled a gaping void.

These days, in good weather, people looking to buy local form two-hour lines outside to wait for tables. The renaissance is slowly taking over the whole block as Cooley is converting nearby empty buildings into condos and artists' studios. This takes less money than one might imagine; when we drove around the day after that lunch, Cooley pointed out a 30,000-square-foot building he'd made a $100,000 offer on. In New York, you can't get 300 square feet for $100,000. Applied strategically, a little capital and effort goes a long way. I could see that, as we hiked over a muddy yard into what looked like a totally abandoned house. Cooley explained that this house was another of his projects—and pointed out the intricate pattern of wood on the walls. A local artist had created a walk-through art installation in what looked like a squatter's camp. As Cooley told me, and clearly believes, "there's tremendous potential everywhere."

The net result of all this civic investment is that Cooley gets to know people from all over Detroit and the world, because everyone brings out-of-town guests like me to Slows. Locals want to show visitors a distinctively Detroit experience. You can't do that at Applebee's. He gets to know people in Detroit's art scene as he renovates studios, and meets other civic-minded folks during neighborhood beautification projects (which have the added side effect of making the scenery outside Slows a little nicer). Cooley's investment in Slows is making him wealthy in the traditional sense—the restaurant did

$1.8 million in sales in its first year, the *New York Times* has reported, and kept growing from there—but beyond that, creating 105 desperately needed new jobs at two locations in Detroit, and a flourishing neighborhood, is making him wealthier in a much broader sense. Cooley's money has created a community he'd want to live in.

Even if you can't start a Slows, you can eat in the equivalent in your town and help support the unique institutions that people will want to visit. More visitors means more money coming in, which has spillover benefits for people in other professions. "We as a society are overinvested in huge, behemoth companies," says Jessica Jackley, ProFounder's cofounder (and a founder of Kiva, through which people give microloans to entrepreneurs in the developing world). "When you invest in small businesses, you know you're doing something specific and direct and good for your community." And often, that community winds up doing something direct and good for you as well.

ALL THE
MONEY IN
THE WORLD

CHAPTER 10

Ode to a Ziploc Bag

I swear the S.C. Johnson company did not pay me to say this, but I adore Ziploc bags.

When I was growing up, my siblings and I brought our lunches to school most days, which meant my family went through an astonishing quantity of sandwich bags. For economy's sake we usually used some generic kind that we had to fold over or secure with a twist tie. I imagine my parents felt there wasn't much difference between these and Ziploc bags, and they preferred to spend their money on other things. I didn't think much about it either, until the fall of 2006, when new airport security measures, enacted after a foiled transatlantic bomb plot, foisted Ziploc bags onto the public consciousness. Suddenly, passengers had to stash carry-on toiletries in clear zip-top bags. I tried out a Ziploc on a November trip to a friend's destination wedding and . . . wow.

Have you ever pondered how wonderful these little bags really are? The plastic is nice and thick. You can see what's in there, but the zip closure keeps everything secure— even loose items like Cheerios,

or damp items like diaper wipes. As soon as I started packing my toiletries in these bags, I was hooked. I would take handfuls from those
piles they'd give away in airports for people who forgot the rules and
tried to carry their toothpaste through security. I'd hoard and reuse
them until my makeup turned the bags grimy and my razors started
poking holes through the plastic.

And then, about two years ago as I was rinsing out one of my
well-worn Ziploc bags, a thought popped into my head: I could *buy*
these things.

This may seem blindingly obvious, but many of us learn our habits young. Parents have a lot less say over children's long-term success
than we like to think, but random preferences seem to get transmit-
ted like eye color. I have always picked pickles off the hamburgers I
order in restaurants because this is what the rest of my family did—as
though pickles are something you'd clearly throw away, like the
toothpick holding the hamburger together. Likewise, I learned from
my early days in the shopping cart seat that generic sandwich bags
are perfectly fine. And so, the first time I pulled a package of Ziploc
brand bags off the shelf, and paid the extra $2 for the privilege of
having them, it felt terribly decadent. I tried to go through the package as slowly as possible, eking out the maximum pleasure possible
from this splurge.

My husband doesn't have the same hang-ups in the grocery store.
Elsewhere, yes. It can take years for him to retire frayed dress shirts
from his wardrobe, but he is pretty fearless about spending money on
groceries. Consequently, on one of our Costco runs after my initial
bag splurge, we wound up with a whole case of hundreds, or possibly
thousands, of Ziploc bags in our cupboards. Every time I pulled one
out and saw the copious volume remaining, I got a little thrill.

But here's the question: how long will I feel this thrill? I worry it's
starting to wane a bit, even now. When we came back from a drive
the other day, with 10 semi-crushed pretzels left in a bag, I did not

throw the pretzels away and save the bag. I just chucked the whole thing. Ten years from now, I may not even think about my Ziploc bags anymore. I'll come to expect them. As will my children, who may pull the pricey branded item off the shelves without even pondering if the extra cost is worth it in terms of their personal satisfaction.

Researchers call this phenomenon the hedonic treadmill. According to the theory, as people make more money, their expectations rise in tandem. If you never go out to eat, the mere experience of sitting in a booth at T.G.I. Friday's can be the height of bliss. If you go out to eat a lot, you soon notice that every restaurant serves some version of meat, fish, chicken, and pasta. You need Michelin stars to look forward to your meal.

We've spent this book exploring how we can use money to buy happiness, namely by using it to foster experiences or create space in our lives for the things that matter. But is there a point at which our ability to spend money on the things we say we want no longer brings us the satisfaction it once did? As we use money to create happiness in our lives, will it eventually take more of it to keep us at that same state of contentment? Will it eventually take all the money in the world to buy our satisfaction? Or is there any way to step off the hedonic treadmill once in a while or slow it down so we can still celebrate life's little luxuries like Ziploc bags or name-brand toothpaste? Perhaps most critically, is there any way to raise our children to appreciate the value of a dollar without imposing an austerity that we, as parents, spent years working hard to escape?

It's not easy. There are probably finer lines than we imagine between teaching kids to be smart with money vs. tight with money vs. wasteful with it. But I do think there is something to be said for teaching a sense of abundance along with the usual fears—namely, that there's never enough.

THE ETERNAL CLIMB

We live in a society where the usual story—the one we expect—is that people will do better, financially, over time. We expect children to do better than their parents. Sometimes much better. In 2007, Oprah Winfrey told graduating seniors at Howard University that her grandmother's fervent wish for her was that she'd work for some "good white folks" who treated their household help well. The punch line is that there are lots of good white folks (and others) tripping over themselves to work for this self-made billionaire. Or take the story of President Barack Obama, whose single mother raised him in often thin circumstances. He went on to become the most powerful man in the world.

Millions of stories are less extreme. I spent big chunks of the summer of 2010 hiking around New York City researching the decline of Korean greengrocers for *City Journal*—a story that turns out to be one of economic success. Korean immigrants came to the United States in the 1970s and 1980s and, facing discrimination in the labor market, decided to open their own businesses. Working in delis and groceries was tough, dangerous work, but it gave them an economic foothold in America as they pushed their children to succeed academically. The children rose to their parents' expectations, with the result that second-generation Korean Americans are now working as doctors, professors, and civil servants, rather than selling lottery tickets in delis that are open 24 hours a day.

Of course, anecdotes don't mean anything on their own. Some statistics show that economic mobility has declined in the United States in the last few decades and is less here than in many other developed nations. Winfrey and Obama notwithstanding, intergenerational mobility is unfortunately less common in the modern African American experience than for white Americans. Data from the Economic Policy Institute's "State of Working America" report finds that of African American children born in the lowest income quartile, 62.9 percent remained there as adults. Only 3.6 percent made it to the top 25 percent. Among white children, though, being born into a lower-income family is far less of a sentence. Only 32.3 percent of white children born in the lowest quartile stayed there, and a full 14.2 percent made it to the top. Nonetheless, an early 2011 *Washington Post* poll found majorities of Americans of all colors think we are doing better than our parents: 51 percent of whites, 53 percent of blacks, and 52 percent of Hispanics, vs. 19 percent in all three racial brackets who think we're doing worse. More of us believe our children will do better than we have than believe the opposite. Surprisingly, among African Americans, a full 60 percent thought their children would have a better standard of living, and only 18 percent thought they'd do worse—a far more optimistic view of the universe than white parents held (36 vs. 31 percent). Even if the statistics don't show an encouraging amount of upward mobility, we believe it exists.

The hedonic treadmill is a pretty fundamental part of this belief in the eternal climb. Economists even have to build it into their data for calculating the cost of living. Think about it. If you just got up between chapters to get a glass of water, did you marvel that clean water shows up in your house without your having to do anything? Such a feat would have been a major quality-of-life improvement for most households 150 years ago. Now, we notice it only in its absence. The fact that we expect children to survive infancy is another hedonic adaptation I think we're quite happy to have gotten used to.

But the hedonic treadmill is a tricky phenomenon. Plenty of surveys have found that women are not as happy now as they were 50 years ago. Certain traditionalists cite this as evidence that we all want to be waxing our floors rather than climbing the corporate ranks, but the treadmill is also about changing frames of reference. Once, perhaps, women compared themselves with other women.

Now, we compare ourselves to men, and with the heightened expectations of burgeoning opportunities, not just any men, but masters-of-the-universe men in corner offices. The hedonic treadmill makes us less or at best equally happy, even as we have more and more. We get used to any state and return to our previous happiness levels.

I can see this in my own life. The first time one of my columns appeared in *USA Today*, when I was a 22-year-old intern, I think I rounded up every copy of that issue in the entire Washington, D.C., area. Ten years and a hundred columns later, I keep one or at most two copies of these clips for my files. As for my finances, I was on track to do better than I ever thought I would on my own. And then, at age 24, I met a nice man in a bar—a business-y type 10 years my senior who turned out to be doing better. When I married him, this introduced an added twist to my life that I hadn't really anticipated and eventually led me to ask this question: If one *can* purchase many of the goods or experiences that consumer culture dictates one should want, how does one continue to find pleasure in little things?

Some research has found that, in fact, exposure to money does make it harder to enjoy small pleasures. One paper published in *Psychological Science* in 2010 measured the effect of income or exposure to money on happiness and savoring positive emotions. Broad surveys found negative effects, the authors noted, and more intriguingly, when study participants in Canada were exposed to pictures of money, they spent less time savoring the chocolate bars they were then given, and appeared to enjoy them less. It is the cruel irony of human existence. We want things we cannot have, and once we can have them we no longer want them. Pablo Picasso explained it best when he said "I'd like to live as a poor man with lots of money."

So how does one do that? It's a mind-set I'd love to have and am trying to cultivate—to be constantly excited by new experiences or little wins. In my case, my temperamental cheapness has helped make that a possibility. If it took me years to get over my hang-up about buying Ziploc bags, that suggests I'm not about to develop a fetish for designer shoes, or if I do, it will take decades to bloom. Having small children has also helped slow the hedonic treadmill in that it makes many of life's luxuries that I could theoretically afford, such as eating out and child-free traveling, logistically more difficult. I do these things, but I do them less than I would without kids. When I do, they are new treats all over again. Once you've survived a plane flight with a newly potty-trained three-year-old and a screaming baby, reading a magazine on a business trip to Akron feels like a day at the spa. Also, since I'd rather spend any given hour writing than shopping, I'm rarely in stores seeing what things my money could buy.

Even if you're not temperamentally cheap, though, and don't have small children, the best approach for maintaining enjoyment of small pleasures seems to be reminding ourselves that they are just that: pleasures. The research on gratitude has probably been over-hyped, but there's little harm in training the mind to seek the good in simple things. The shape of a toddler's button nose. A functioning computer. A sunny day. Nice-smelling shampoo. A good cup of coffee. All can pass without notice or can be noticed, written down, and celebrated.

None of this is rocket science, though I find it ironic how big an industry "simplicity" has become. There's a reason *Real Simple* magazine has that title, as opposed to "Real Easy" or "Real Quick," even though there's nothing real simple about $400 linen pants and other such items that make it into the magazine's fashion spreads. We are constantly searching for narratives that make sense, and escaping the clutter and chaos of modern life, finding happiness in such nonmaterial things as smelling the flowers, hits all the right notes. And so, it's important to remember with the hedonic treadmill that it's not all bad. We *should* expect running water and kids that don't starve, and it's a sign of progress that we view the lack of a cell phone as deprivation, as opposed to *real* deprivation.

WHAT DO I TEACH MY KIDS?

I think *Real Simple*'s $400 linen pants offer an intriguing insight into our love-hate relationship with the treadmill—an insight with implications for parenting. We decry our materialistic society, but we don't want true austerity. We extol simple, homemade foods . . . but not the cheap and sugary Jell-O salads that our less wealthy great-grandmothers cranked out. I am willing to live on much less than we make in the interest of broader financial goals, but there are limits. I'm not willing to live in a bad neighborhood or resurrect the ramen-noodle-cooking skills I learned during my intern days, unless I really have a craving for ramen noodles.

My kids will see this, and so I've been struggling lately to figure out what I should teach them about money. The Internet is full of tips, and many—I soon discovered—aren't based on any research whatsoever. So to learn more, I interviewed Lewis Mandell, dean emeritus of SUNY Buffalo's School of Management. Mandell has studied the topic of children and money for years, and notes that "it's just amazing to me . . . There are people out there who are experts on children and write books on children and tell us all these things as if they're accepted gospel, and it's totally unsubstantiated by any kind of data, or any kind of surveys."

For instance, should kids get an allowance? It seems like a straightforward way to teach them how to manage money. Give them $5–$10 a week, and let them handle their small purchases out of that. Likewise, financial education for high schoolers sounds smart. Given the proportion of adults who live paycheck to paycheck and don't understand what the interest rates on their credit cards mean in terms of payments, it can't hurt to teach kids about money.

But as we saw in the chapter on the marginal cost of kids, people are far too complicated to have any one input lead inexorably to a certain outcome. Mandell's research, he tells me, has found that children who received regular allowances that were not conditional (i.e., given as payment for chores) were less likely to demonstrate financial savvy than children who got paid for chores *and* children who received no regular allowance money at all. Analyses of multiple allowance studies suggest that "nonconditional allowances made kids feel entitled," says Mandell. "They're associated with a lower inherent desire to work." Kids "seem to feel that money just appears without any effort going into it." In theory, children who have to ask their parents for spending money would also see that money appears without work, but if you think about it, constantly negotiating for money is kind of a job, too. "I compare those kids with someone who works for a living as a development officer at a nonprofit," Mandell says. "They go in every day and ask for money." You start to think about what is worth bothering with and what is not, and you spend time thinking through the arguments. Whereas perhaps kids who get a nonconditional allowance come to believe (as many grown-ups do) that there's always another payday around the corner as long as you show up. Money becomes mindless over time.

Likewise, Mandell has found that teens who take even high-quality financial education classes don't score better on financial literacy tests. Later on, they're no less likely to carry credit card balances or bounce checks. "The courses made no difference whatsoever," Mandell says. He speculates that—unlike driving techniques learned in driver's ed—much of financial education is not immediately useful to a 17-year-old. It will be a few years before most apply for a mortgage, and even those who are earning a regular paycheck are seldom solely responsible for maintaining a household out of that check. So, as with trigonometry, we forget what's covered immediately after the final exam. When it comes time to actually use this information, we figure out what we need (or want to know) from other sources, rather than what we learned in class.

So what are we to make of this? A few things seem more likely to matter. As with my pickles and generic bags, children do learn habits from their parents, even in the absence of any specific financial lessons.

Behavioral psychologist Matt Wallaert is the former lead scientist at Thrive, an online personalized financial service. "I talked to literally thousands of people about personal finances," he said. "Never in my entire time did I find anyone who was really good with money who didn't say, 'I learned it from my parents.'" If your children see you paying your bills on time, living on less than you make, and putting money away for the future, this becomes the norm. If your young children have savings accounts and simply learn that a percentage of birthday and holiday money always goes there, this will be an incredibly difficult habit to break later on. Saving will feel like brushing their teeth. Mandell speculates that one other reason, beyond lack of relevancy, that high school financial literacy classes don't help is that kids have picked up their deepest beliefs long before then. Any true intervention has to come around ages 8 to 12 to shape someone's mind-set. That still doesn't mean it will work. We all know children of frugal parents who can blow through far more cash than they could ever personally accumulate, but the younger the better.

My blog readers and other experts I interviewed had all sorts of tips (though some debated Mandell's allowance findings). The best centered on being open about your finances, so kids don't come to see money as a secretive thing. Use relatives' financial woes as teachable moments. Use TV as a teachable moment. "TV has some of the best teachable moments ever," says Shay Olivarria, a financial education speaker and author. If kids are watching shows they shouldn't be watching (e.g. MTV's *Cribs*), then "at least get something good out of it," she says. Why do the characters think that a flashy house or car indicates success? Talk about why a lower interest rate on a mortgage matters in terms of monthly payments, and if you're working extra hours to afford a particular vacation or to get out of debt, make sure they see the connection. Keep in mind that in a cashless culture, kids may have a harder time grasping what money really is. "A lot of children don't understand how ATM cards work," says Olivarria. "They think it's magic. They don't understand that money has to go in the bank for you to pull money out of the bank." They may think that when you want something, you just swipe a card and get it, without understanding that a bank balance is debited somewhere, or that you'll have to pay a credit card bill later. So it may be worth using cash on occasion to help them understand what's going on. Also, feel free to let them fail. Olivarria enjoys taking her nephews, nieces, and cousins to the amusement parks near her California home. She gives them a set amount of cash (say, $20) and tells them they have to use it for food and any other desires. Inevitably, the first time a child has cash in hand, he blows it on a plush toy in the first five minutes and then has to suffer through a long day of watching his siblings eat hamburgers and ice cream and buy other souvenirs with their carefully stewarded money. "That is an awesome lesson," says Olivarria. "I'd rather let an eight-year-old go hungry at Disneyland because he blew his money on a plush Mickey than have a thirty-year-old blow money on something and now his kids are homeless."

Whether they get an allowance or not, encourage your children to figure out their values as they start to earn their own money through babysitting, lawn mowing, or a teenage part-time job. Talk about taxes, and why we pay them, and how rates are set. One of my blog readers, Leah, noted that her family's finances were a totally open book to her after age 16 because her father, who ran his own business, officially made her his bookkeeper. She struggled to learn QuickBooks and made costly errors, but "as my confidence and skill grew, it became an even enjoyable task," she writes. "I kept up this 'job' for my parents until I married at age 23." A teenager can be put in charge of online bill paying with some supervision; you'll know she's learned the ins and outs of money management when she puts you on a strict Christmas budget instead of asking for everything under the sun.

Of course, part of this process is figuring out your own beliefs about money. I'm still struggling with this. When I began pondering what I would teach my children, my first instinctive thought was that I wanted them to "know the value of a dollar." I do think there is great freedom in living within your means and building up savings, and in having the discipline to say no to things so you can say yes to larger goals. I've read my fair share of horror stories of grown-up young adults racking up credit card debt and expecting their parents to bail them out, because they simply don't understand or respect what it takes to earn the cash that they fritter away. I would definitely be sad if my children refused to work hard or ever viewed certain kinds of work as beneath them. We have narratives we like to tell ourselves about lousy early jobs—that "it's not what you earn it's what you learn." We like to believe they build character.

Then again, sometimes I question what I learned in my lousy jobs. As I mentioned in chapter 3, I spent one teenage summer ladling garlic butter over breadsticks at Fazoli's Italian fast food restaurant for eight hours a day to the point where I smelled so bad I had to open the windows on the drive home to air out. I spent a semester of college delivering newspapers at 6:30 A.M. while my more well-funded classmates slept in. These jobs taught me something. But at least one of the lessons I learned is that I really don't have the heart to force my children to do such jobs just to build character. These days, I'd be more likely to tell them to learn a useful skill. My little brother knew how to program computers and build Web sites and consequently never had to ladle butter.

The fact that I know the value of a dollar has also led me to make shortsighted choices because I sometimes value those dollars too much—falling toward that "love of money" hole no less than an overspender would. I held out on hiring as much child care as we needed because it was expensive, but this made it harder to build my career and put a lot of strain on my marriage. I've been reluctant to invest in the business side of my work, by hiring assistants or paying for publicity, because I tell myself I could "save" money by doing it myself. Except then it gets done badly or (more often) doesn't get done. I hope I could teach my children that frugality is not a virtue in its own right, divorced from any larger goal. Money is powerful not because of anything inherent in these numbers, but because of what it can do. Sometimes we have to take risks, and sometimes we should invest in things that matter.

These thoughts are also influenced by my realization that spending money on children isn't just about making them happy. It's about making *us* happy. As we learned in the chapter on giving, spending money on other people—even strangers—produces higher utility than spending money on yourself. It would follow that spending money on people you love to the point of distraction would produce even higher utility. We do it on Christmas and birthdays. What's wrong with doing it some other times, too?

I raised this issue on my blog in light of a dilemma I faced in Barnes & Noble one Saturday morning not long ago. Jasper and I had gone for a run and to run errands (meaning I had gone for a run with him in the jog stroller) while Michael stayed with the baby. I love spending one-on-one time with Jasper, especially as he is getting older and is able to communicate more intriguing thoughts. We had a great time talking to each other and enjoyed a surprisingly warm and sunny late fall day. He was even good in the grocery store, despite the epic Trader Joe's line. As I'd promised him at the beginning of the day, I took him to the bookstore. We read several books together, and then he found the Thomas and Friends toy display.

I don't know why so many toys are being sold in what is ostensibly a bookstore, but I do know this: we have been obsessed with the wooden Thomas trains for quite a while. Jasper saw Gordon (the long blue express engine, for those of you without preschoolers) and his tender (coal car), and he asked for it.

What should I do?

I decided to buy Gordon quickly—a rather pricey impulse purchase at $21.99. Then after my haste, I repented at leisure, pondering what I had just done. Was I spoiling my child? Viewed in the light of earning $4.90 an hour at Fazoli's, purchasing Gordon and his tender would require five hours of unpleasant labor. All that to buy a little toy train just like the 10 other toy trains my son had at home (though not Gordon, as he told me in the bookstore, which turned out to be correct).

Of course, the reason he has 10 of them is that life has gotten better since those $4.90/hour days. As choreographer Twyla Tharp wrote in her memoir, *The Creative Habit*, "once your basic needs are taken care of, money is there to be used." In my head, and later on my blog, I ticked through the reasons that it was okay to drop $21.99 on a spontaneous gift for my son. My retirement account is funded. I have an emergency fund that could last me a long time. My kids have college funds, and we all have health insurance. If we've been responsible on all those fronts, what's wrong with having fun with my money? The night before the Gordon purchase, my husband and brother and I spent more than $21.99 on margaritas at a Mexican restaurant because quaffing them was fun. So why not spend the same on Jasper's whims? There are few things more enjoyable than listening to my three-year-old babble all day about how "Mommy and me had fun at the bookstore! And we got Gordon!" Stuff doesn't make us happy, but stuff you really play with turns into an experience. I am editing this chapter several months after the bookstore trip, and I can attest that Jasper (and as he's gotten older, Sam) still plays with Gordon and his other trains close to every day. That's pretty good for your average toy and three-year-old.

My blog readers found my hand-wringing funny and offered some words of reassurance.

Diana wrote that I should "Stop feeling so guilty. The kid is three! He is not even capable of learning (or caring) about 401(k) funding or health insurance. And he shouldn't have to. He knows nothing about any of those things. He knows Gordon. And he loves him. If you bought it because you wanted to buy it for him, that's one thing. If you bought it because you were afraid of a tantrum in the bookstore, that's entirely different. I doubt that he felt entitled. He just really wanted Gordon. And you had the means to get it for him and you did. The end."

Likewise, Miles wrote, "Of course money can't buy love. And we want to teach our kids all the important things. But we also want to just shower them with love, and sometimes that means spending frivolous money on them because they want something. If you do it all the time, that's likely a problem." (I don't; the other day we went to the drugstore without my purchasing any of the candy Jasper pointed toward.) "But sometimes you just need to be extravagant. Parenting (like life in general) is a mixture of body, mind, and soul—the physical, the mental, and the emotional. All are necessary ways of expressing love. Don't let fear rule you. 'Perfect love casts out fear.' While that means something different in its full context, it turns out to be an excellent general principle."

Perfect love casts out fear—fear that we won't have enough, and fear that (love of money being the root of all evil) the plenty we do have will somehow harm these precious creatures. I hope to avoid erring in either direction. The other day I found Jasper carefully putting his toys into our Ziploc bags. So at least for now, he still seems to think they're pretty neat. In the absence of deprivation—perhaps even with all the money in the world—one can still model enthusiasm for all the joys of life.

THE HOW TO BUY HAPPINESS HANDBOOK

All the Money in the World aims to make you think differently about the resources you have or could get. How can money help you create the life you want? I've compiled some of the exercises from the book here, along with questions to ask yourself, or to discuss in a book group, investment club, coffee klatch, or wherever you talk about money. I invite you to share your answers with me and other readers via my Web site, www.all-the-money.com, which is part of www.LauraVanderkam.com.

PART 1: THE BIG PICTURE

---

1. If you had all the money in the world—not literally, but all you wanted—how would you change your life?

Personal pet peeves you might resolve: _____

_____

_____

Personal aspirations you'd attempt: _____

_____

_____

Broader goals you'd support: _____

_____

_____

2. Could you make progress on any of these fronts with less than all the money in the world? How much, specifically, would you need? Are any of these important enough to you to become long-term financial goals?

3. Even if you had all the money in the world, what would you *not* want to spend money on?

4. The Reckoning

Look at your bills and receipts for a representative period (a month tends to give people a good sense of their general habits, though even a day is helpful). Write them down and rate how you felt about each (1 = mad, 2 = annoyed, 3 = neutral, 4 = happy, 5 = thrilled)

_____	1	2	3	4	5
_____	1	2	3	4	5
_____	1	2	3	4	5
_____	1	2	3	4	5
_____	1	2	3	4	5
_____	1	2	3	4	5
_____	1	2	3	4	5
_____	1	2	3	4	5
_____	1	2	3	4	5
_____	1	2	3	4	5

	1	2	3	4	5
_____	1	2	3	4	5
_____	1	2	3	4	5
_____	1	2	3	4	5
_____	1	2	3	4	5

What are you happiest to spend money on? What does this tell you about your values?

5. The $10,000 Question

Say you got a $50,000 inheritance. You put the first $40,000 toward savings, retiring debts, or your usual charitable commitments. The remaining $10,000 is fun money. What would you do with it? The only rule is that you'd need to look back on your life and think you'd spent the money well. List several ideas. Compare yours with friends' ideas and vote on which you like the best.

Looking for inspiration? I'll be writing stories at www.all-the-money.com about people who have done something from their $10,000 list. The experience needs to be memorable and creative, and you can't have incurred any debt to do it. Write me via the Web site with details.

PART 2: GETTING

1. How do you feel about your income? Are you underpaid, fairly paid, or overpaid? What about other members of your household? Why do you think you earn what you earn?

2. What is your definition of rich?

3. If you wanted to earn an extra $2,000 by the end of next month, what could you do?

4. If you wanted to boost your family's income by 25 percent over the next two years, what could you do?

5. What if you wanted to double your income? (If you succeed, I'd love to profile you for an ongoing feature on people who've changed their income dramatically. Write me via www.all-the-money.com.)

6. What is your minimum wage? That is, how much do you need to earn per hour for any frugal practice to be worthwhile? What wage are you earning from any frugal practices you do now?

7. How much do you think you'd need in your "freedom fund"—or in regular investment income—to never have to work again? How much would you need in order to not work for two years?

8. If you didn't have to work, what would you want to do with your life? Give yourself one to two years off for travel or other leisure pursuits. What would you want to do after that? Picture yourself on a Monday morning in as much detail as possible.

9. Can you incorporate any elements of that scenario into your current work? If you gave yourself two years, what could you change?

PART 3: SPENDING

1. What percentage of your budget goes toward housing and transportation? Does this feel right? If you lowered this by 10 percentage points, what would you do with the extra cash?

2. If your income was cut in half, would you still be able to afford your basic expenses?

3. How would your family cope if you could have only one car?

4. How many items do you think you own?

5. Are there any items you could share in common with neighbors, friends, or extended family?

6. Looking at your possessions, which do you consider your best purchases ever? (Write me with details for an ongoing feature on the purchases that have made people happiest).

7. What would it cost to create a weekend you'd want to repeat again and again (a "Groundhog Weekend")?

Ask yourself four questions:

▶ **What activities do you enjoy most?** List five ideas here. If any seem unaffordable, think of ways you could have a similar experience for less.

_____ Cheap version: _____	
_____ Cheap version: _____	
_____ Cheap version: _____	
_____ Cheap version: _____	
_____ Cheap version: _____	

▶ **When, exactly, can you plan these?** Pick an upcoming weekend, and schedule them into slots. What arrangements do you need to make ahead of time?

Friday evening:

Saturday day:

Saturday evening:

Sunday day:

Sunday evening:

Arrangements to make _____

_____

_____

_____

_____

_____

▶ **How can you off-load the not-fun stuff?** Can you create a small block of time for chores, errands, and anything else you don't want to do? Or, better yet, can you ignore, minimize, or outsource these tasks?

▶ **What is this costing you and how do you feel?** Keep a spending and feelings diary during your weekend. That way, in the future, you'll know for sure what will boost your spirits and exactly what that will cost.

Please write me with the details of your Groundhog Weekend and how you pulled it off. I'll also feature these stories on my blog.

8. Do you think the marginal cost of children declines? What trade-offs would you make if you had a larger family? How would your spending patterns change if you had a smaller family?

9. If you had all the money in the world (not literally, but all you wanted), would you change what you spend on your children? Why? What do you think that would change about their lives?

10. What are you teaching your children about money? What did you learn from your parents? What money habits of yours do you hope your children will pick up, and which do you hope they won't?

11. What do you do best that other people can't do nearly as well? Which activities bring you the most joy? List some of your core competencies.

12. How could you use money to clear other things off your plate, so you could focus more time on these core competencies?

PART 4: SHARING

1. What causes really motivate you? When you skim a newspaper, what kinds of articles draw you in? What communities have you visited or lived in that you'd like to improve? What do you credit as a turning moment in your life? What issue *really* ticks you off? For ideas, try browsing Web sites such as DonorsChoose.org and Global Giving.org.

2. What percent of your income do you currently devote to "pro-social" spending—gifts and charity?

3. What kind of need or opportunity would cause you to double that?

4. How can you give the bulk of your charitable dollars in a way that builds and strengthens social ties for you?

5. Give yourself a pot of philanthropy fun money. What are some ways you could make the world better for $5–$20? Check them off when you've tried them. Please e-mail me via my Web site with stories about "Random Acts of Microphilanthropy" to share some of them with other people.

6. How could you use your time or money to support entrepreneurs and job creation in your community?

7. The $1,750 question: Figuring a pay rate of $17.50 per hour, what would you do with 100 hours of someone's time? What nagging tasks would you take care of if you just had another set of hands? Are there any tasks you could outsource that might help you boost your income and/or life satisfaction over time?

8. If you planned to shop with a mission—turning your community into a distinctive and attractive place—which stores would you start

frequenting? What would you buy? What are you better off getting at a chain store or online?

9. Is it possible to "live as a poor man with lots of money"? How could you do that?

10. Are you better off than your parents or grandparents? Do you think your children will be better off than you?

ACKNOWLEDGMENTS

Book projects are solitary endeavors in some ways, but the more of them I survive, the more I learn how much it helps to have a team at work and at home.

My editor, Brooke Carey, yet again shepherded a book from vague idea to finished form—in this case, a far more vague idea than with *168 Hours*. I would not have been able to go from a one-page outline and a contract for a book called "Untitled on Money" to an actual book without her editorial guidance. Thanks to the Portfolio team of Adrian Zackheim, Will Weisser, Amanda Pritzker, Tiffany Liao, and the rest for their continued support for my writing—and especially for their skill in turning random musings into marketable concepts—and to Emilie Stewart for negotiating all these projects.

Thanks to John Siniff and Glen Nishimura at *USA Today* for publishing several op-eds on subjects in this book, to Pam Kruger at BNET, the team at *City Journal*, Siobhan O'Connor at *Prevention*, and Lisa Belkin with her *New York Times* blog Motherlode for letting me test-drive chunks of this material. Thanks to the readers of the

My168hours.com blog for offering their feedback, and especially to my "beta readers" who waded through this manuscript in its earlier versions and offered tips on making it more readable and useful. Thanks to Nancy Sheed for developing the "Just a Minute" newsletter and helping with publicity and social media so I could concentrate on writing.

A particular thanks to all the people who agreed to be interviewed for *All the Money in the World*. Sharing details about one's finances (and one's life in general) with a journalist is always nerve-racking, and I am grateful for the trust I have been given.

Writing books is time-consuming business and requires a lot of support on the home front as well. My husband, Michael Conway, has taught me to spend more at the grocery store and to ask for more money in negotiations. His weekend excursions with our little ones have given me extra quiet hours to work; I am not sure how many other preschoolers and toddlers have gotten to experience the campiness of the Coney Island Mermaid Parade while their mom is racing to meet a book deadline, but extra edification is one of the benefits of having a dad with an adventurous streak. Thanks to Kathryn, Carrie, Lauren; my mother-in-law, Diane; and my parents, Jim and Mary, for all the care they've given our children over the past few years and the contributions they've made to keeping our home running smoothly. As for the kids themselves—Jasper, Sam, and their eagerly awaited sister Ruth—they haven't exactly boosted my productivity in a traditional sense. But they give me such fodder that I'm always grateful for my adorable little distractions. Whatever the marginal cost of these kids turns out to be (see chapter 6), I am grateful for having them in my life.

NOTES

INTRODUCTION: YOU HAVE MORE MONEY
THAN YOU THINK

3 *A handful of Dutch researchers once set up a test:* Quoted in *The Economist*, March 31, 2011, www.economist.com/node/18483423.

4 *One classic example from the literature:* J. Riis, G. Loewenstein, J. Baron, C. Jepson, A. Fagerlin, and P. A. Ubel (2005), "Ignorance of hedonic adaptation to hemodialysis: A study using ecological momentary assessment," *Journal of Experimental Psychology: General* 134, no. 1: 3–9. As mentioned in Sonja Lyubomirsky, *The How of Happiness* (New York: Penguin, 2007).

9 *According to 2006 figures from the UN's World Institute for Development:* United Nations University, World Institute for Development Economics Research, "Pioneering study shows richest two percent own half world wealth," December 5, 2006, www.wider.unu.edu/events/past-events/2006-events/en_GB/05122006/.

9 *In 2007, the median net worth for U.S. households:* U.S. Census Bureau, "Income, Expenditures, Poverty and Wealth," *Statistical Abstract of the United States, 2011*, Table 720, "Family Net Worth." Available at www.census.gov/compendia/statab/2011/tables/11s0720.pdf.

CHAPTER 1: WHAT ELSE COULD THAT RING BUY?

16 *According to statistics from TheKnot.com's annual Real Weddings survey:* "The Knot unveils 2010 real weddings survey results," March 2, 2011, www.theknotinc.com/

pressreleaseshome/2011pressreleases/201103022011realweddingssurveyresults. aspx.

17 *Like this gem from* Money: Walter L. Updegrave, "Getting ready to prosper in the '90s," *Money Extra,* Fall 1988, 26.

17 *In a 1990 article for the* Journal of Law, Economics & Organization: Margaret F. Brinig, "Rings and promises," *Journal of Law, Economics, & Organization* 6 (1990): 203. Available at http://homes.chass.utoronto.ca/~siow/332/rings.pdf.

20 *That is, "once you find the person":* Bowman is quoted in Laura Vanderkam, "What else could that ring buy?" *USA Today,* February 10, 2010.

21 *Yet one* Redbook *poll found that:* "Do you do date nights?" *Redbook,* February 2010, 90.

21 *With the same $5,392 the average couple spends on an engagement ring:* All numbers in subsequent paragraphs from The Knot Real Weddings survey, March 2, 2011.

23 *You get used to having won the lottery:* P. Brickman, D. Coates, and R. Janoff-Bulman (1978), "Lottery winners and accident victims: Is happiness relative?" *Journal of Personality and Social Psychology* 36: 917–27.

23 *You get used to being married:* R. E. Lucas, A. E. Clark, Y. Georgellis, and D. Diener (2003), "Reexamining adaptation and the set point model of happiness: Reactions to changes in marital status," *Journal of Personality and Social Psychology* 84: 527–39.

23 *Yet as Sonja Lyubomirsky, a professor of psychology:* Sonja Lyubomirsky, *The How of Happiness: A Scientific Approach to Getting the Life You Want* (New York: Penguin, 2007), 65.

25 *According to the BLS, the average American household:* Bureau of Labor Statistics, Consumer Expenditures 2009, published October 5, 2010, and available at www .bls.gov/news.release/cesan.nr0.htm.

25 *To see how you stack up against people more like you:* All statistics from Bundle.com, "Everybody's Money" section, which will change as more people input numbers.

27 *One 2008 Gallup poll found that 51 percent of employed Americans:* Dennis Jacobe, "Half of Americans say they are underpaid," Gallup.com, August 18, 2008, www.gallup.com/poll/109618/halfamericanssaytheyunderpaid.aspx.

27 *One study, published in* Science *in 2004:* Daniel Kahneman, Alan B. Krueger, David A. Schkade, Norbert Schwarz, and Arthur A. Stone (2004), "A survey method for characterizing daily life experience: The day reconstruction method," *Science* 306 (5702): 1776–80.

CHAPTER 2: DON'T SCRIMP MORE, MAKE MORE

36 *According to statistics from Nielsen, coupon "enthusiasts":* Todd Hale, "The coupon comeback," Nielsen Wire, April 13, 2010, http://blog.nielsen.com/nielsenwire/ consumer/thecouponcomeback/?utm_campaign=Feed%3A+NielsenWire+%2 8Nielsen+Wire%29.

36 *There's a story called "Ode to His Frugal Wife":* Thomas J. Stanley and William D. Danko, *The Millionaire Next Door* (New York: Pocket Books, 2000) 44–45. Originally published in 1996.

36   *as Betty Friedan described it in* The Feminine Mystique: Betty Friedan, *The Feminine Mystique* (New York: Dell, 1977) 36. First published in 1963.

38   *In 2010, psychologist Daniel Kahneman and economist Angus Deaton:* D. Kahneman and A. Deaton, "High income improves evaluation of life but not emotional well-being," *Proceedings of the National Academy of Sciences* 107, no. 38 (Sept. 21, 2010): 16489–93.

41   *A few years ago,* Forbes *magazine crunched some numbers:* "How Americans make and spend their money," Forbes.com July 19, 2006, www.forbes.com/2006/07/19/cx_de_americanspending_9.html?thisSpeed=6000.

41   *A 2009 CareerBuilder.com survey:* "Six-in-ten workers live paycheck to paycheck, reveals new CareerBuilder survey," September 16, 2009, www.careerbuilder.com/share/aboutus/pressreleasesdetail.aspx?id=pr525&sd=9%2F16%2F2009&ed=12%2F31%2F2009.

41   *The Federal Reserve conducts surveys every three years:* Brian K. Bucks et al., "Changes in U.S. family finances from 2004 to 2007: Evidence from the survey of consumer finances," *Federal Reserve Bulletin,* February 2009. Available at www.federalreserve.gov/pubs/bulletin/2009/pdf/scf09.pdf.

42   *"the majority of people do not have the ability to increase their incomes . . .":* Stanley and Danko, *Millionaire Next Door,* 163.

42   *Scrolling through the Bureau of Labor Statistics':* BLS, "May 2010 National Occupational Employment and Wage Estimates," www.bls.gov/oes/current/oes_nat.htm.

44   *In February 2011, Louise Tutelian wrote a piece for CBS's MoneyWatch.com:* "Dream jobs: Six-figure salaries and a bright future," Louise Tutelian, February 28, 2011, http://moneywatch.bnet.com/careeradvice/article/sixfigurejobsmobileapplicationsdeveloper/6197976/.

45   *Households in the top income quintile have an average of about two income earners:* See census figures here: www.census.gov/hhes/www/cpstables/032010/hhinc/new05_000.htm. Those in the top 5 percent are also far more likely to have two income earners than one.

45   *Economist Sylvia Ann Hewlett's research on "off-ramping" finds:* Sylvia Ann Hewlett, *Off-Ramps and On-Ramps: Keeping Talented Women on the Road to Success,* (Boston: Harvard Business School Press, 2007), 46.

45   *A variety of surveys, including some from the Pew Research Center:* Kim Parker, "The harried life of the working mother," Pew Research Center, October 1, 2009, http://pewsocialtrends.org/2009/10/01/theharriedlifeoftheworkingmother/.

45   *Warren Farrell, author of* Why Men Earn More: Interview with author.

46   *down to the 19 hours per week the American Time Use Survey finds:* BLS, "American Time Use Survey, Married Parents' Use of Time," May 8, 2008, www.bls.gov/news.release/atus2.t02.htm.

46   *According to Linda Babcock and Sara Laschever's 2003 book:* Linda Babcock and Sara Laschever, *Women Don't Ask: Negotiation and the Gender Divide* (Princeton, NJ: Princeton University Press, 2003).

47   *one paper published by the National Bureau of Economic Research:* A. Lusardi, D. Schneider, and P. Tufano, "Financially fragile households: Evidence and implications," NBER Working Paper No. 17072, issued May 2011.

49   *And with 26 percent of the U.S. workforce identifying themselves as free agents:* "Freelance

ranks growing as economy is slowing, Kelly Services survey shows," Kelly Services Inc., January 28, 2009, http://ir.kellyservices.com/releasedetail.cfm?releaseid=361950.

50   *with Etsy sales rising from $88 million:* For Etsy sales stats see: www.etsy.com/press/kit/.

55   *The average household spends 7.6 percent of its budget on food consumed:* Bureau of Labor Statistics, "Consumer Expenditures, 2009," www.bls.gov/news.release/cesan.nr0.htm.

56   *Dave Lassman, vice president of operations at Leed's:* Laura Vanderkam, "5 signs it's time to hire," BNET, January 27, 2011, www.bnet.com/blog/timemanagement/5signsit8217stimetohire/217.

CHAPTER 3: RETHINK RETIREMENT

60   *Judith Van Ginkel is 72:* Laura Vanderkam, "Not your grandfather's retirement," *USA Today,* January 4, 2011.

61   *According to the Bureau of Labor Statistics, after decades of decline:* BLS, "Spotlight on Statistics, Older Workers," July 2008, www.bls.gov/spotlight/2008/older_workers/.

61   *This brought the labor force participation rate among people over age 65:* BLS Employment Projects, "Civilian labor force participation rates by age, sex, race, and ethnicity," published in November 2009 *Monthly Labor Review* and available at www.bls.gov/emp/ep_table_303.htm.

61   *One study published in the* Journal of Occupational Health Psychology *in 2009:* Y. Zhan, M. Wang, Songqi Liu, and K. Shultz, "Bridge employment and retirees' health: A longitudinal investigation," *Journal of Occupational Health Psychology* 14, no. 4 *(*2009): 374–89.

63   *As a young intern at* Fortune *during the summer of 2000:* Carolyn Geer, "Ready, set, quit," *Fortune,* August 14, 2000.

64   *As Janice Revell wrote in the 2002 follow-up article:* Janice Revell, "Best-laid plans," *Fortune,* August 12, 2002.

66   *the Social Security Administration is a bit touchy about this point:* In response to a "frequently asked question" about 1930s life expectancy, the SSA has created a page on "Life expectancy for Social Security," explaining issues of infant mortality and demographics. Their explanation and tables are available here: www.ssa.gov/history/lifeexpect.html.

67   *In Dave Ramsey's* The Total Money Makeover: Dave Ramsey, *The Total Money Makeover: A Proven Plan For Financial Fitness* (Nashville, TN: Thomas Nelson, 2009), 156, 159. Originally published in 2003.

67   *In* The Automatic Millionaire, *personal finance guru David Bach:* David Bach, *The Automatic Millionaire: A Powerful One-Step Plan to Live and Finish Rich* (New York: Broadway Books, 2004). Chart is on p. 48 in the paperback edition.

69   *A 1988* Money *magazine article on where to invest in the 1990s:* The economist A. Gary Shilling predicted that the Dow would rise to 5,000 or 6,000 by the end of the decade. See Walter L. Updegrave, "Getting ready to prosper in the '90s," *Money Extra,* Fall 1988, 32.

70   *In 2011, EBRI found:* Employee Benefits Research Institute, "Retirement Confi-
      dence Survey, 2011." RCS Fact Sheet #2, "Preparing for Retirement in Amer-
      ica," is available at www.ebri.org/files/FS2_RCS11_Prepare_FINAL.pdf. Fact
      Sheet #3, "Age Comparisons Among Workers," is available at www.ebri.org/
      files/FS3_RCS11_Age_FINAL.pdf.

71   *Surveys of Americans find that two thirds of adults say they would continue to work:* Scott
      Highhouse, Michael J. Zickar, and Maya Yankelevich, "Would you work if you
      won the lottery? Tracking changes in the American work ethic," *Journal of Ap-
      plied Psychology* 95, no. 2 (March 2010): 349–57. This percentage has declined
      from 80 percent in the 1950s but seems to have leveled off at around two thirds.

74   *As Suzanne Braun Levine, a cofounder of* Ms. *magazine:* Talk given as part of a *New
      York Times* Knowledge Network course, presented by Civic Ventures, October
      29, 2010.

75   *In* The Creative Habit, *choreographer Twyla Tharp writes:* Twyla Tharp, *The Cre-
      ative Habit: Learn It and Use It for Life* (New York: Simon & Schuster, 2006), 137
      (paperback edition).

76   *According to a 2007 McKinsey Consumer Retirement Survey:* "Winning the Retirement
      Race: The McKinsey & Company Consumer Retirement Survey 2007," avail-
      able at www.mckinsey.com/clientservice/financialservices/pdf/Winning_the_
      Retirement_Race.pdf.

76   *Andrew Biggs, former principal deputy commissioner:* See Laura Vanderkam, "This
      isn't grandpa's retirement," *USA Today,* January 4, 2011.

77   *R. Albert Mohler Jr., president of the Southern Baptist Theological Seminary:* Albert
      Mohler, "For the sake of the kingdom: Redefining retirement," January 6,
      2011, www.albertmohler.com/2011/01/06/forthesakeofthekingdomredefining
      retirement/.

79   *Robert Pondiscio worked as the communications director for* BusinessWeek: For the full
      story of his teaching and career change, see Robert Pondiscio, "'Mr. P' learns
      his lesson," *BusinessWeek,* December 6, 2007, www.businessweek.com/magazine/
      content/07_51/b4063202308685.htm.

80   *But here's something she did want to do: pay cash for a house:* Based on an interview with
      Crystal Paine, and also her series on this goal, "Saving 100 percent down for
      our first home," December 31, 2009—July 8, 2010, http://moneysavingmom
      .com/saving100downforourfirsthome.

CHAPTER 4: LAUGHING AT THE JONESES

85   *cartoonist Arthur R. Momand surveyed his Long Island neighbors:* For one profile, see
      Alex Jay's February 16, 2011, write-up of "Pop" Momand at comic strip histo-
      rian Allan Holtz's Web site, Stripper's Guide, http://strippersguide.blogspot
      .com/2011/02/popmomandprofiledbyalexjay.html.

86   *And so, in 2009, the average American family spent:* BLS, "Consumer Expenditure
      Survey, 2009."

86   *according to 2006 numbers from* Forbes: Laurence H. M. Holland and David M.
      Ewalt, "How Americans make and spend their money," Forbes.com, July 19,

2006, www.forbes.com/2006/07/19/spendingincomelevel_cx_lh_de_0719 spending.html.

89 an "axiomatic good," as Time magazine put it: Barbara Kiviat, "The case against home ownership," Time, Sept. 11 2010.

89 The most popular reasons for home ownership: "New nationwide survey provides comprehensive look at sentiment toward housing," Fannie Mae, April 6, 2010, www .fanniemae.com/newsreleases/2010/4989.jhtml.

90 There is some research, often touted by real estate agents: Kiviat, "The case against home ownership."

90 big chunks of us—some two thirds of Americans—buy: U.S. Census Bureau, "Residential vacancies and homeownership in the first quarter," April 27, 2011, available at www.census.gov/hhes/www/housing/hvs/qtr111/files/q111press.pdf.

92 while new single-family homes in the early 1970s: U.S. Census Bureau, "Median and average square feet of floor area in new single-family houses completed by location," available at www.census.gov/const/C25Ann/sftotalmedavgsqft.pdf.

92 The median price rose from: U.S. Census Bureau, "Median and average sales prices of new homes sold in United States," available at www.census.gov/const/us priceann.pdf.

92 Financial writer Liz Pulliam Weston: Liz Weston, "Don't bite off too much house," MSN Money, December 20, 2009.

93 The average commute is now hovering at about 50 minutes per day: U.S. Census Bureau, 2009 American Community Survey, "United States—commuting characteristics by sex," http://factfinder.census.gov/servlet/STTable?_bm=y&geo_ id=01000US&qr_name=ACS_2009_1YR_G00_S0801&ds_name=ACS_ 2009_1YR_G00_&_lang=en&redoLog=false&format=&CONTEXT=st.

93 According to a 1–10 scale of human happiness: John P. Robinson and Geoffrey Godbey, Time for Life: The Surprising Ways Americans Use Their Time (University Park: Pennsylvania State University Press, 1997). See p. 340, "Ratings of detailed activities on enjoyment scale (1985 diaries)."

93 In the 2004 study of Texas working women: Daniel Kahneman, Alan B. Krueger, David A. Schkade, Norbert Schwarz, and Arthur A. Stone (2004), "A survey method for characterizing daily life experience: The day reconstruction method," Science 306, no. 5702: 1776–80.

94 Some economists such as Robert Frank: Robert H. Frank, Falling Behind: How Rising Inequality Harms the Middle Class (Berkeley and Los Angeles: University of California Press, 2007).

94 In a 2010 paper surveying dozens of experiments: Elizabeth W. Dunn, Daniel T. Gilbert, and Timothy D. Wilson, "If money doesn't make you happy, you probably aren't spending it right," November 12, 2010, available at http://dunn.psych .ubc.ca/files/2010/12/ifmoneydoesntmakeyouhappy.Nov1220101.pdf.

96 Fannie Mae found a slight decrease: www.fanniemae.com/media/pdf/2011/Housing SurveyFactSheetq12011.pdf.

97 A summer 2010 survey from real estate listing service: Trulia American Dream Survey, Trulia-Harris Interactive Survey conducted July 22–26, 2010, http://info.trulia .com/index.php?s=43&item=96.

97 By 2009, the average new home size: U.S. Census Bureau, "Median and average square feet of floor area."

101 *Consider the story of Diane Faulkner:* See Laura Vanderkam, "Out of fashion: Green lawns," *USA Today*, August 17, 2010.

102 *By some estimates, maintaining nonnative plants:* From interview with Audubon Society for above *USA Today* column.

104 *Tom Vanderbilt's fascinating 2008 book,* Traffic: Tom Vanderbilt, *Traffic: Why We Drive the Way We Do (and What It Says About Us)* (New York: Knopf, 2008).

CHAPTER 5: THE BEST WEEKEND EVER

111 *she took just 34 things:* Nina Yau, Castles in the Air, February 6, 2011, http://castles intheair.org/blog/34things/.

115 *The study I keep referencing of Texas working women:* Kahneman et al., "A survey method for characterizing daily life experience."

115 *A variety of studies find that we enjoy exercise more in the fresh air:* J. Thompson Coon, K. Boddy, K. Stein, R. Whear, J. Barton, and M. H. Depledge (2011), "Does participating in physical activity in outdoor natural environments have a greater effect on physical and mental well-being than physical activity indoors? A systematic review," *Environmental Science & Technology* 45, no. 5:1761–72. DOI: 10.1021/es102947t.

116 *As I was writing an article for* Prevention *on this topic:* Laura Vanderkam, "Love your weekends again!" *Prevention,* June 2011, 89–91.

117 *Indeed, research published in the journal* Applied Research in Quality of Life: Nawijn et al., "Vacationers happier, but most not happier after a holiday," *Applied Research in Quality of Life*, March 2010, 5, no. 1: 35–47.

CHAPTER 6: THE MARGINAL COST OF CHILDREN

123 *More than 80 percent of Americans will have at least one child:* See Jane Lawler Dye, "Fertility of American women, 2008," U.S. Census Bureau, available at www .census.gov/prod/2010pubs/p20563.pdf.

124 *those who have studied the relative happiness of parents:* One study that originally demonstrated this connection was Luis Angeles, "Children and life satisfaction," *Journal of Happiness Studies*, published online October 14, 2009, available at www. unav.es/icf/main/top/noviembre09/Angeles_Felicidadmatrimoniohijos.pdf, but this was later retracted when Angeles discovered a calculation error: http:// www.springerlink.com/content/l725601150537035/fulltext.pdf.

124 *A 2003 Gallup poll that surveyed childless adults:* Frank Newport, "Desire to Have Children Alive and Well in America," The Gallup Poll, August 19, 2003. Available at http://www.gallup.com/poll/9091/desire-children-alive-well-america. aspx.

125 *according to 2008 census numbers, among women aged 40–44:* "Fertility of American Women, 2008."

125 *In 2010, the median house price in the United States was:* U.S. Census Bureau, "Me-

dian and average sales prices of new homes sold in United States," available at www.census.gov/const/uspriceann.pdf.

125 *the U.S. Department of Agriculture produced a report claiming that it cost*: Mark Lino (2010), "Expenditures on children by families, 2009," U.S. Department of Agriculture, Center for Nutrition Policy and Promotion, Miscellaneous Publication No. 1528-2009. See p. 26, table 1, for the $222,360 number for middle-income families. Available at: www.cnpp.usda.gov/publications/crc/crc2009.pdf.

126 *In 2009, the USDA reported, a two-parent family:* Ibid. See p. 16, table 8.

127 *In early 2011, Lisa Belkin, then with the* New York Times: Lisa Belkin, "The marginal cost of children," February 8, 2011, NYTimes.com, http://parenting .blogs.nytimes.com/2011/02/08/themarginalcostofchildren/.

129 *Some recent studies have debunked most popular prejudices about only children:* See Lauren Sandler, "The only child: debunking the myths," *Time,* July 8, 2010, www.time .com/time/nation/article/0,8599,2002382,00.html.

134 *This is what economist (and Nobel laureate) Gary Becker famously argued:* Gary S. Becker and H. Gregg Lewis, "Interaction between quantity and quality of children," published in *Economics of the Family: Marriage, Children and Human Capital,* 1974 (an out-of-print publication of the National Bureau of Economic Research). Available at: www.nber.org/chapters/c2963.pdf.

134 *reduction in fertility in poor communities*: For a good discussion of this topic, see Abhijit V. Banerjee and Esther Duflo, "Pak Sudarno's Big Family," chapter 5 in *Poor Economics: A Radical Rethinking of the Way to Fight Global Poverty* (New York: Public Affairs, 2011). Surveying evidence from China, Bangladesh, and elsewhere, the authors write that "there is no smoking gun to prove that larger families are bad for children."

136 *A recent American Enterprise Institute analysis of schools, grouped by selectivity:* Frederick M. Hess, Mark Schneider, Kevin Carey, and Andrew P. Kelly, "Diplomas and dropouts: Which colleges actually graduate their students (and which don't)," American Enterprise Institute, June 2009. Available at www.aei.org/docLib/ Diplomas%20and%20Dropouts%20final.pdf

137 *If your family earns up to $180,000 per year, Harvard now charges:* "Harvard Financial Aid Fact Sheet, Academic Year 2010–2011," available at http://isites.harvard .edu/fs/docs/icb.topic551531.files/Financial%20Aid%20Fact%20Sheet.pdf.

137 *The* Wall Street Journal *publishes an annual list of the top schools where corporate recruiters*: Teri Evans, "Penn State tops recruiter rankings," *WSJ,* Sept. 13, 2010, http://online.wsj.com/article/SB10001424052748704358904575477643369663352.html.

138 *Some 70 percent of high school graduates now enroll in college:* BLS, "College enrollment and work activity of 2010 high school graduates," April 8, 2011, www.bls.gov/ news.release/hsgec.nr0.htm. The figure was 68.1 percent for 2010.

138 *Bryan Caplan's 2011 book:* Bryan Caplan, *Selfish Reasons to Have More Kids: Why Being a Great Parent Is Less Work and More Fun Than You Think* (New York: Basic Books, 2011).

139 *At-home mothers spend a bit more time playing with their kids:* American Time Use Survey, Married Parents' Use of Time, www.bls.gov/news.release/atus2.t02.htm.

139 *But CDC research has found that young children at home with a parent:* Centers for Disease Control and Prevention, "Television and video viewing time among chil-

dren aged 2 years—Oregon, 2006–2007," published in *Morbidity and Mortality Weekly Report*, July 16, 2010, www.cdc.gov/mmwr/preview/mmwrhtml/mm5927a1.htm.

CHAPTER 7: THE CHICKEN MYSTIQUE

142 *chronicled in Shannon Hayes's:* Shannon Hayes, *Radical Homemakers: Reclaiming Domesticity from a Consumer Culture* (Richmondville, NY: Left to Write Press, 2010).

145 *The March 2011 issue of* Martha Stewart Living: Susan Heeger, "Southern comfort," *Martha Stewart Living*, March 2011, 106–13.

145 *gardening supply company W. Atlee Burpee & Co.:* Bruce Horovitz, "Recession grows interest in seeds, vegetable gardening," *USA Today*, February 20, 2009.

145 *Barbara Kingsolver made such agrarian practices sound enticing:* Barbara Kingsolver, Camille Kingsolver, and Steven L. Hopp, *Animal, Vegetable, Miracle: A Year of Food Life* (New York: Harper Collins, 2007).

149 *"Money becomes a marginal chit":* Hayes, *Radical Homemakers*, 5.

149 *"Mainstream Americans have lost the simple domestic skills . . .":* Ibid., 12.

150 *"the cost of a thing is the amount of what I will call life . . .":* Henry David Thoreau, *Walden; or Life in the Woods*, first published in 1854.

156 *"the center for social change . . .":* Hayes, *Radical Homemakers*, 18.

CHAPTER 8: THE SELFISH JOY OF GIVING

161 *For a 2008 paper published in* Science: Elizabeth W. Dunn, Lara B. Aknin, and Michael I. Norton, "Spending money on others promotes happiness," *Science* 319 (March 2008).

163 *read a cover story in the* New York Times: John W. Fountain, "In trenches of a war on unyielding poverty," *New York Times*, September 29, 2002.

166 *Back in February 1979,* Forbes *magazine:* James Cook, "Is charity obsolete?" *Forbes*, February 5, 1979.

167 *Individual Americans gave $227.41 billion in 2009:* "U.S. charitable giving falls 3.6 percent in 2009 to $303.75 billion," The Center on Philanthropy at Indiana University, June 9, 2010, www.philanthropy.iupui.edu/news/2010/06/prGUSA2010.aspx.

167 *I spent some time walking the streets of Seattle:* Laura Vanderkam, "Give them homes," *USA Today*, April 28, 2008.

168 *"There's a lot of evidence that this generation . . .":* Quotes are from Laura Vanderkam, "Microphilanthropy is changing the face of charity," *USA Today*, November 18, 2010.

171 *according to Charity Navigator, from 2004 to 2008:* Numbers received directly from Charity Navigator.

176 *perhaps this is what Al Gore was thinking:* For one (of many) mentions, see Judith Havemann, "GOP labels Al Gore a 'Scrooge,'" *Washington Post*, April 17, 1998.

176 *The average person gives roughly 3 percent:* This varies slightly by income group. Working-class Americans are slightly more generous (4.5 percent of income) than middle-income (2.5 percent) and upper-income Americans (3 percent). See Arthur Brooks, "A nation of givers," *The American,* March/April 2008.

177 *A reader signed up for a financial makeover with expert Liz Pulliam Weston:* For the saga of Beth, see "The money fix: Beth's $30,000 adoption," October 20, 2010, www .dailyworth.com/blog/583TheMoneyFixBeths30000Adoption. The follow-up is "The money fix: Beth's internal budget battle," November 8, 2010, www.daily worth.com/blog/597themoneyfixbethsinternalbudgetbattle.

182 *as a Pittsburgh group called Here You Go:* Anya Sostek, "Umbrella program may spawn bumper crop of good deeds," *Pittsburgh Post-Gazette,* April 24, 2010.

CHAPTER 9: ANOTHER WAY TO INVEST

183 *I was mostly there to interview Margarita:* Laura Vanderkam, "Entrepreneurs feed Detroit's extreme makeover," *USA Today,* March 8, 2011.

186 *according to statistics from the Kauffman Foundation:* Tim Kane, "The importance of startups in job creation and job destruction," Ewing Marion Kauffman Foundation, July 2010. Available at www.kauffman.org/uploadedFiles/firm_formation_ importance_of_startups.pdf.

187 *In the deepest days of the recession in late 2009:* American Express OPEN Small Business Monitor, September 17, 2009, available at http://media.nucleus.naprojects .com/pdf/American_Express_OPEN_Small_Business_Monitor.pdf.

187 *it feels "absolutely amazing" to make a hire:* Laura Vanderkam, "5 signs it's time to hire," BNET, January 27, 2011.

188 *If you're worth millions:* See the SEC's definition of "accredited investor" here: www.sec.gov/answers/accred.htm.

188 *More than 5 million U.S. households:* "Hawaii tops millionaires per capita," Phoenix Marketing International, September 29, 2010, www.phoenixmi.com/index .php/site/story_content/?company_id=1522.

188 *Wealth patterns being what they are:* Laura Vanderkam, "Venture capitalists, it's time to invest in women," *USA Today,* April 26, 2011.

188 *Women own close to one third of all U.S. businesses:* The American Express OPEN State of Women-Owned Businesses Report, available at http://media.nucleus .naprojects.com/pdf/WomanReport_FINAL.pdf.

188 *But women-owned businesses receive well under 10 percent:* John R. Becker-Blease and Jeffrey E. Sohl, "Do women-owned businesses have equal access to angel capital?" *Journal of Business Venturing,* Elsevier, 22, no. 4 (July 2007): 503–21.

189 *Two years later, it has raised $40 million:* Yancey Strickler, "Happy birthday Kickstarter!" The Kickstarter blog, April 28, 2011.

190 *So the reasons for contributing are mixed:* Laura Vanderkam, "Grads, 'crowdfund' a career," *USA Today,* June 8, 2011.

190 *In 2010, Regan Wann:* RocketHub project listing for "Moving through the looking glass," www.rockethub.com/projects/113movingthroughthelookingglass.

191 *BucketFeet, a company that makes "wearable art" sneakers:* David Lang, "Case study:

BucketFeet," Profounder, January 24, 2011, http://blog.profounder.com/2011/01/24/casestudybucketfeetflatoutcool/.

191 *in June 2011, the* Wall Street Journal *reported*: Angus Loten, "Peer-to-peer loans grow," *Wall Street Journal,* June 16, 2011.

192 *while reading a tongue-in-cheek column Joel Stein:* Joel Stein, "Why $1700 means Joel Stein is rich," *Time,* October 10, 2010.

195 *in 2004, research firm Civic Economics:* "The Andersonville study of retail economics," Civic Economics, October 2004, available at www.civiceconomics.com/AndersonvilleStudy.pdf.

195 *Civic Economics confirmed the direction of this difference:* "Local Works! Examining the impact of local business on the West Michigan economy," Civic Economics, September 2008, available at www.civiceconomics.com/GR_Local_Works_Complete.pdf.

198 *the restaurant did $1.8 million in sales in its first year:* Melena Ryzik, "Detroit's renewal, slow-cooked," *New York Times,* October 19, 2010.

CHAPTER 10: ODE TO A ZIPLOC BAG

206 *In 2007, Oprah Winfrey told graduating seniors at Howard*: For the full text of her 2007 speech, see www.graduationwisdom.com/speeches/0024winfrey.htm.

206 *researching the decline of Korean greengrocers:* Laura Vanderkam, "Where did the Korean greengrocers go?" *City Journal* 21, no. 1 (Winter 2011).

206 *Data from the Economic Policy Institute's "State of Working America":* See chart, "Mobility differs by race," www.stateofworkingamerica.org/charts/view/229. Cited from Tom Hertz (2006), "Understanding mobility in America," Center for American Progress.

207 *Nonetheless, an early 2011* Washington Post *poll found:* Peyton M. Craighill, "Behind the numbers—Will your children be better off? Results from the race & recession poll," *Washington Post,* February 21, 2011, http://voices.washingtonpost.com/behindthenumbers/2011/02/judging_standard_of_living_for.html.

207 *Plenty of surveys have found that women are not as happy:* For one discussion, see Betsey Stevenson and Justin Wolfers, "The paradox of declining female happiness," *American Economic Journal: Economic Policy, 2009* 1, no. 2: 190–225.

208 *One paper published in* Psychological Science: J. Quoidbach, E. W. Dunn, K. V. Petrides, and M. Mikolajczak, "Money giveth, money taketh away: the dual effect of wealth on happiness," *Psychological Science* 21, no. 6 (June 2010): 759–63.

216 *As choreographer Twyla Tharp wrote in her memoir:* Twyla Tharp, *The Creative Habit,* 32.

INDEX